Friends

On the cover tissue of the Quaker folio is the single faint word "Friends," which rubbed off the title page.

AUGUST EDOUART: A QUAKER ALBUM

Augustin Amant Constant Fidèle Edouart
(actual size)
1789–1861

Silhouette self-portrait of Edouart cut on his return to France in 1849. He is holding a diamond-studded snuff box given to him by the Emperor of Austria.

AUGUST EDOUART
A Quaker Album

*AMERICAN AND ENGLISH
DUPLICATE SILHOUETTES 1827–1845*

Helen and Nel Laughon

Foreword by Wendell Garrett, editor and publisher
The Magazine Antiques

CHESWICK PRESS
RICHMOND, VIRGINIA 1987

ORIGINAL ALBUM IN THE COLLECTION
FRIENDS HISTORICAL LIBRARY OF SWARTHMORE COLLEGE

Copyright © 1987 by Helen and Nel Laughon
Library of Congress Cataloging-in-Publication Data
Laughon, Helen, 1919–
  August Edouart: a Quaker album of American and English duplicate silhouettes, 1827–1845
  Bibliography: p. 109
  Includes index.
  1. Quakers—United States—Portraits. 2. Quakers—England—Portraits. 3. Edouart, Augustin-Amant-Constant-Fidèle, 1789–1861. 4. Silhouettes—United States. 5. Silhouettes—England. 6. Quakers—United States—Genealogy. 7. Quakers—England—Genealogy. I. Laughon, Nel, 1946–   . II. Title.
  E184.F89L38 1987   973′.088286   86-9689

ISBN 0-9616686-0-1

No part of this book may be reproduced or transmitted in any form or by any means, electronic or mechanical, including photocopy, recording or any storage and retrieval system now known or to be invented, without permission in writing from the publisher, except by a reviewer who wishes to quote brief passages in connection with a review written for inclusion in a magazine, newspaper, or broadcast.

Inquiries should be addressed to Cheswick Press, 8106 Three Chopt Road, Richmond, Virginia 23229.

First Edition

Printed in the United States of America

Cover: Miss Ellen H. Lea and Richard M. Lea. These children are found in the conversational group of the Lea family. Duplicates are on page 170 of the Quaker duplicate section and the framed and finished silhouette which is now in a private collection is on page 117.

Designed by Geary & Flynn Design, Inc.

Contents

Prologue by August Edouart   vii

Foreword by Wendell Garrett   ix

"American Quaker in Profile" by Eleanore Price Mather   xi

"The Significance of Styles of Dress within the Religious Society of Friends" by Joan Kendall   xiii

Introduction by Helen and Nel Laughon   1

Advantages of Duplicates   13

Quaker Duplicate Book   15

Index of Sitters   109

Framed and Finished   114

Acknowledgements   119

Select Bibliography   121

Daniel Trimble
(actual size)

This is a duplicate of Mr. Trimble. The original is in the finished picture in The Winterthur Museum, Inc. Collection. Other family members, page 60 and 60½, also appear in this finished family group.

Prologue

To speak concerning my labours, I shall give an idea of them: the names of the persons I take, and the dates, are written five times over—first, on the duplicate of the Likeness—secondly, in my day book—thirdly, in the book in which I preserve them—fourthly, in the index of that book—and fifthly, in the general index. This much in itself is a hard task to fulfil. Without this arrangement, how could I, at a minute's notice tell, whether I had taken the Likeness of any person enquired for, and could it be otherwise possible, to produce the Silhouette.

Augustin Amant Constant Fidèle Edouart, *A Treatise on Silhouette Likeness by Monsieur Edouart, Silhouettist to the French Royal Family and patronized by His Royal Highness the Duke of Gloucester, and the Principal Nobility of England, Scotland, and Ireland* (London: Longman; Cork: Bolster; Edinburgh; Fraser, 1835) p. 98.

Ann H. Mabbett
Camilla E. McCarty

(actual size)

These young ladies from New York were cut in May of 1840 and can be found on folio page 44 1/2. Ann is carrying a "prop" doll and Camilla the family cat.

Foreword

Every student and reader of History, who strives earnestly to conceive for himself what manner of Fact and Man this or the other vague Historical Name can have been, will, as the first and directest indication of all, search eagerly for a Portrait, for all the reasonable Portraits there are; and never rest till he have made out, if possible, what the man's natural face was like. . . . I have found that the Portrait was as a small lighted candle by which the Biographies could for the first time be read, and some human interpretation be made of them.

Thomas Carlyle to David Laing on the "Project of a National Exhibition of Scottish Portraits," May 3, 1854.

The Society of Friends and its members—the Quakers—have played a crucial role in American history. In England they learned to live as an embattled minority among others who thought differently from them; but in the New World their ideas and institutions assumed decisive importance as they learned to be a people among peoples. The exciting adventure of William Penn's Holy Experiment in Pennsylvania became something of a laboratory for testing the founder's plans for a colony where religious freedom, representative government, cheap land, and feudal proprietary arrangements would furnish a haven for poor and oppressed peoples and an example of enlightened government for the world; it also became a populous antecedent of America's pluralistic society.

The Friends lived lives of strict Quaker ways and lofty ideals, and believed that they had the capacity individually to cultivate "that good seed universally sown in every heart, by the great and good Husbandman." They rejected pride, greed, and worldliness, and they decried superfluity in dress, furniture, and manners. They were a plain people who warmly endorsed sobriety, Sabbatarianism, practical piety in doing good to fellow men, and the strict use of Quaker speech. They met at Quaker meetings for worship in a plainly furnished room, wearing unornamented clothes of an old-fashioned cut, most of the men sitting on one side, women on the other, both facing the front benches on which sat the dignitaries of the meeting. From time to time someone broke the silent waiting with a prayer or with an exhortation to virtuous living. The distinctive tenet of Friends was the belief in the Inner Light—meekness, purity, and intense religious experience.

But after the American Revolution pious Quakers began to realize that lax discipline and doctrinal deviation were creeping into Quaker religious life; many historic traditions of Quaker heritage were being compromised with the world. Devout Quakers sounded lamentations and protest against the growing attachment to ease, wealth, and respectability—a gradual and subtle transformation of the Quaker spirit, a change that has been designated a shift in concern from the meetinghouse to the countinghouse. Despite these latter-day compromises and the subsequent decline of Quaker piety in the early nineteenth century, the rigorous ethical discipline of Penn's Holy Experiment contributed to the commercial success of the City of Brotherly Love. Despite the rapid growth of the non-Quaker population, the Quaker merchant princes and political leaders continued to dominate the life of the city and the Keystone State. During the early decades of the nineteenth century, when Pennsylvania would become a crossroads of the nation, it would also remain a world center of Quaker influence. During the decade of the 1840s the artist Augustin Edouart cut the silhouettes of the Friends in this volume, which happily are so numerous as almost to furnish us a candelabrum (and that of high candlepower) of historical portraits of some Pennsylvania Quakers. Each portrait is in fact a historical document, a primary source of importance to the student of history; these in the composite bring light where light is sorely needed, and show us who are but the shadows, the reality that was a sect among sects, of a truly remarkable people among peoples.

Wendell Garrett

Benjamin Willmore
(actual size)

He was taken on October 6, 1827 in Cheltenham, England and is the earliest duplicate mounted in this folio.

American Quakers In Profile

The seventeenth-century missionary activity of the Society of Friends and the persecution that it provoked left little time for portraiture. After Quaker settlement in the New World brought prosperity some portraits by Hesselius (Gustavus and son John), Claypoole (James, 1720–1798), and Copley were commissioned by the very affluent, but the bias against such canvases remained strong. Their time-taking sittings suggested too much of creaturely concern, encouraging vanity and extravagance.

In the later years of the eighteenth century the technique of profile taking appealed to the thrifty Quakers. It offered speed and cheapness, and avoided color—by this time frowned upon in dress and furnishings. And at the amateur level the process provided an innocent pastime in the wholesome atmosphere of the home.

Prominent among amateurs was Joseph Sansom (1767–1826), of Philadelphia, whose silhouettes, preserved in the Perot Collection at the Historical Society of Pennsylvania, were painted rather than cut. Not only did he present a galaxy of Quaker worthies, but also such public figures as Washington, Franklin, James Madison, and Robert Morris, who walked the streets of William Penn's city in the 1790s when it was the nation's capital. Sansom shared the Friends' traditional interest in the Indian, and painted a seated figure of Red Jacket, Chief Speaker of the Five Nations, whose fringed buckskins strike an exotic note among the neat caps and broadbrims of the collection.

Quakerism also produced a distinguished professional silhouettist in William Henry Brown (1808–1882), of Charleston, South Carolina, who ranged the eastern seaboard portraying many celebrities. But none, it would seem, were Friends.

It remained for the great French master, Augustin Edouart, to record in profile the American Quakerism of the 1840s. It was a curious combination—this rapport between a former Napoleonic soldier and a culture that not only forbade military service, but also such recreations as cards, theater, dancing, and racing. As Anna Cox Brinton points out in her delightful *Quaker Profiles, Pictorial and Biographical, 1750–1850* (Wallingford, Pa.: Pendle Hill Publications, 1964), the century between 1750 and 1850 "was the period when Quakers were most clearly distinguishable from others by their speech, dress, and behavior."

But these very restrictions may explain the empathy between the French émigré and the Quakers. For their world was one of discipline, which he probably understood and respected, rendering their orderly regime with the same scrupulous care that his sitters lived it.

His exquisite touch with the scissors found willing patrons in the areas of New York, Baltimore, Wilmington, and Philadelphia. Most were city dwellers, living in sedate brick houses with white marble steps in front and ample gardens in the rear—hence the flowers in the hands of many of the younger women. Some were involved in social concerns, such as Isaac Hopper (page 56½), and Lucretia Mott, who was also one of the founders of Swarthmore College (page 116). On the same page with Lucretia and her husband appears Elias Hicks, the most notable Friends' minister of his time. Edouart copied this from a wood engraving issued by John Hopper (son of the above Isaac), possibly from a print in the collection of Thomas Gilpin, now in the Friends Historical Library at Swarthmore. A gifted amateur, Gilpin was a warm friend of the French artist, who portrays both him and Hopper in the present volume (pages 140 and 56).

Elsewhere the artist delights in the children of the Charles and Richard Wood families as they sport with their toys (pages 122 and 123), in the highly social dog extending a paw at Sarah Pennock's tea party (page 149), and in young Cheesman and his sister Ann, holding violin and guitar respectively—a startling phenomenon in this Quaker realm, where music was still officially taboo (page 80).

In spite of its restrictions American Quakerism was not a somber world. Augustin Edouart captured it, not at its greatest hour, but perhaps at its most charming one, and it has been preserved within these pages.

Eleanore Price Mather

Mrs. Joseph Robinson
Master M. Robinson
Miss Eliza Robinson

(actual size)

In 1836 Edouart was in Limerick and cut the Robinson group. These duplicates are on page 13 in the folio.

The Significance of Styles of Dress within the Religious Society of Friends in England

The Religious Society of Friends, or Quakers as they were nicknamed, emerged during a period of nonconformist evangelism following the Civil War of 1642. The original message preached by George Fox, the founder of the Society, was that Christian qualities are more important than ritual and dogma, and that there should be an awareness of and reliance on the guidance of the indwelling spirit of Christ rather than on the interpretation and intercession of priests. It was a loving and joyful approach to life. "Sing and rejoyce . . . ; for the Lord is at work,"[1] and "then you will come to walk chearfully over the world, answering that of God in everyone."[2]

Friends had a testimony to plainness of speech, behavior, and apparel. The latter was defined as simplicity with no distinguishing marks, for in George Fox's words: "Costly apparrell with ye lace; yt wee formerly had hunge upon our backes yt kept us not warme with yt wee coulde mainetaine a Company of poore people yt had noe cloaths."[3] There was no lack of color in Friends' clothing during the early period; the warnings are all against "superfluities" with no uniform style of dress specified.

Towards the end of the seventeenth century there was an increasing sense in some Friends of their separateness from the world, with a wish for conformity in plainness of dress by maintaining the styles of the founding period. This so concerned Margaret Fox that in the sixth month of 1698 she wrote an epistle to other Friends in which she said,

> It's a dangerous thing to lead young Friends much into the observation of outward things, which may be easily done; for they can soon get into an outward Garb, to be all alike outwardly; but this will not make them true Christians: It's the Spirit that gives Life.[4]

Two years later she wrote,

> In so much that poor Friends is mangled in their minds, that they know not what to Doe: for one Friend says one way, and another, another, But Christ Jesus saith, that we must take no Thought what wee shall Eat, or what wee shall Drink, or what we shall put on: but bidds us consider, the Lilies how they grow in more royalty, then Solomon: But contrary to this, wee must looke at no Collours, nor make any thing that is changable Collours as the hilles are, nor Sell them, nor wear them: But wee must bee all in one Dress, and one Collour; This is a Silly poor Gospell, It is more fitt for us, to be Covered with God's Eternall Spirit, and Cloathed with his Eternal Light, wch Leads us, & Guides us into Righteousness and to live Righteously & Justly & hollyly in this Present evil world.[5]

Many references are found throughout the eighteenth and nineteenth centuries to a current distinctive form of plain Quaker dress recognized as such by non-Friends. There are so many epistles and advices concerning what Friends should *not* wear for one to realize that even from the beginning there were Friends who never adopted the plainest form of dress. These became known as "gay Friends." Strict Friends were called "plain Friends" and there were those who, like George Anne Bellamy (1731–1788), did not dress herself "with the studied formality of a rigid Quaker, but only so plain and neat as to entitle (her) to the denomination of a 'wet Quaker,' a distinction that arises chiefly from the latter's wearing ribbands, gauzes and laces."[6]

Throughout its history, the London Yearly Meeting regularly repeated warnings against following the vain fashions of the world, but many serious and devout Friends felt that an inordinate amount of attention was paid to details of dress, speech, and behavior to the detriment of Spiritual Life. In 1849 a supplement was added to the Rules of Discipline (in practice rules of self-discipline). "We are renewedly persuaded that our testimony to plainness of speech, behaviour and apparel rests upon sound, unalterable grounds."[7]

In the 1850s many pamphlets were written presenting both sides of the disagreement. As the anonymous author of the pamphlet *Nehustan*, said to be Edward Fry, later Lord Justice of Appeal, wrote: "A novelty in dress is first regarded as objectionable, then it is admitted and not considered inconsistant; and lastly, when the rest of men have passed away from it, it is clung to with all the devotion which our Society entertains for its peculiar customs."[8]

At the London Yearly Meeting in 1860 the testimony to plainness was replaced by the advice "Be careful to maintain in your own conduct and encourage in your family that simplicity in deportment and satire . . . which become the disciples of the Lord Jesus."[9]

Plainness lingered on in the Society; plain speech could be heard occasionally during the 1940s and 1950s. Most Friends continue to dress sensibly in simply cut clothes of restrained color and good quality cloth, but there are still those who wear fashionable clothes in lively colors. It is probable that stylized plain dress only lingers now within certain groups of Friends in the United States of America.

One of the "vain fashions of the World"[10] against which Friends testified was that of "making a counterfeit presentment"[11] or having one's portrait painted. This attitude survived to 1929 when the author of *A Mirror for the Society of Friends* wrote, "The present author is under a sense of contrition for reproducing the portraits that illustrate this book. If he has caused any distress of mind thereby he prays to be forgiven."[12]

There are enough uncommissioned portraits of individuals or groups of Friends to show that the colors worn ranged between browns, fawns, sage greens, grays, and creams. Few wore black as this was considered "worldly" and Friends maintained a testimony against mourning.

The introduction of the cutting of silhouettes was acceptable to many Friends because it was an accurate representation of a physical appearance, uninfluenced by the portrait painter's inclination to present a fashionable, possibly flattering, vision of the sitter.

Fashionable dress for women from 1827 for a decade had the greatly exaggerated width of the shoulder line emphasized by the ever-increasing bulk of the sleeves distended by feather-filled pads, stiffened linings, or even whalebone hoops. The naturally placed waistline was tightly compressed, and into this was pleated, or gathered, a skirt that showed the ankles, with the fullness arranged over padding at the back. Hats were enormous and lavishly trimmed, even the bonnets had a very wide brim and a perpendicular crown, and caps were elaborately frilled and gathered. From late in 1836 the shoulder line flattened, the sleeves collapsed in bulk and were inserted low off the shoulder, the bodice lengthened, and the full round skirts descended to the instep. Hats were worn less, bonnets became smaller and their crowns and brims flatter.

The fashionable men of 1827 echoed the women's styles with puffed sleeve heads on narrow-waisted coats that had generous collars and lapels and widely flared skirts. The coats reached to the knee and were worn with trousers. Stocks or high shirt collars and cravats were worn under important waistcoats, and top hats with various heights of crown were usual. About 1837 men's coats became shorter, straighter, longer waisted and less exaggerated in cut, with close-fitting, smooth-headed sleeves and narrower trousers.

When looking at these silhouettes of British Friends one should consider the age and profession or status of the sitter. Some maintained the styles of plain dress they adopted at maturity and others, with a wish not to appear singular, adopted the more discreet forms of current dress.

Nathaniel Hartland (page 8) wears the plain dress of an elderly Friend of this period, a modification of the late-eighteenth century standard dress. That is a plainly cut, calf-length coat with a stand collar, round cuffs, and no pocket flaps, a long single-breasted buttoned waistcoat, knee breeches, stockings, and low shoes with buckles. His wide-brimmed, low-crowned hat is half-cocked with stays and his stick is for support, not show. Moses Goodere (page 7) has a hat without stays and wears a greatcoat with a turndown collar and lapels, which would button across for protection, probably over the same type of clothes as worn by Nathaniel Hartland. It can be assumed that they would also wear a plain shirt with round cuffs and a plain neckcloth tucked into the waistcoat and in inclement weather would add gaiters or wear topboots. Although William Shorthouse (page 20) was represented by description, having died a month earlier, the outline of his hair is that of an eighteenth-century bob wig worn with a nineteenth-century plain coat. Richard Reynolds (page 4), who died in 1816, has a similar outline.

Thomas Simmons (page 11), aged eighty-three, is dressed, however, in one of the plain Friends' current styles, that of a morning coat with the obligatory stand collar, breeches, and a low-crowned top hat. The alternative style was the below-knee-length frock coat with stand collar and trousers of Jacob Allis (page 7). There were slight variations in the cut of the morning coats and Theodore Waterhouse and John Mayfield (page 1), Henry Knight (page 2), and William Cooke (page 19) wear them with trousers. A number of Friends wear gaiters with breeches, notably John Allis Hartland (page 9), and Richard Pim (page 12) wears top boots and spurs. Umbrellas (pages 1 and 9) and walking canes (pages 4 and 11) were used. A white stock, sometimes with the addition of a cravat, was worn.

Degrees of plainness extended from this standard through Joseph Malcomson (page 31) and Joseph Clarke (page 23) with turndown collars on coats of a restrained cut to Edward Strangman (page 14) and William Bell Allen (page 19), who are very stylish.

Of the elderly women Friends, Rebecca Hartland (page 8), aged seventy-nine, wears the muslin cap with a low crown and wideband that would fit under the late-eighteenth-century round bonnet that replaced the long hood and the flat beaver hat worn by earlier women Friends. She wears a neck handkerchief, and the bust after death of Anna Hartland (page 9) shows the same cap shape being worn by a young woman with a small eighteenth-century handkerchief and late-eighteenth-century long skirt shape.

The next development of the bonnet shape can be seen in the caps of Sarah Smith (page 22½) and her daughter Hannah Nutter (page 22) as the bonnet brim lengthens and the gathered crown creeps lower. The gathering at the neck edge of Sarah Smith's cap is shown and the folds of the muslin handkerchief worn over the dress show at the nape. The length of the handkerchief point is clearly shown on Sarah Clarke (page 23) and on Mrs. Thomas Lamb (page 32), who has tied her cap by gathering strings in a definite bow at the back. The plain-fronted, narrow-sleeved gown of Marguerite Harvey (page 36) has an instep-length skirt gathered evenly all around as worn by Miss Goodere (page 7). A triangular, plain-colored, fine-woven woolen shawl, perhaps lined with silk, was worn for warmth. This was usually pinned on the shoulders or at the waist. Its length can be seen on Jane Wakefield (page 15) and on Miss Yerbury (page 2). Shoes were plain and low heeled. Sadly there is no cloak or pelisse shown as an outer garment or any bonnet or oilskin rain cover for a bonnet.

The next development of the bonnet shape can be seen in the cap of Marguerite Harvey (page 36), which fit under the tunnel bonnet of the early nineteenth century and was worn tilted slightly forward with the crown in line with the brim. Her close-sleeve and slightly raised waistline also indicates the early nineteenth century. After this the crown of the cap becomes larger and more sharply angled as with Miss Goodere (page 7) to fit under the fashionable bonnet crown, even when worn with plain dress. Note the long but fashionable flat-fronted and padded-back skirt shape of Mrs. W. Spriggs (page 10) and Mrs. William Nutter (page 22), worn with the handkerchief and fashionable cap with increasingly vertical crown.

A less-plain Friend like Mrs. Joseph Robinson (page 13) wears a collar instead of a handkerchief, but still has a slender sleeve above a fashionable skirt shape and a muslin cap. Both Lucy Clarke (page 19) and Charlotte Dawson (page 34) wear high-necked collars, puffed sleeves, and long skirts. As neither wears a cap, although details of the side hair, whether smooth or in curls, are indistinguishable, the neat bun on the crown of the head is well-defined.

The sleeves become larger as Friends become gayer (Elizabeth Wakefield and Isabella Nicholson Wakefield, page 15), culminating in the highly fashionable skirt length, sleeve puff, low neckline, and pointed cap of Miss Ruth Pim (page 12). The children all wear conventional clothes of the period suitable to their ages with Louisa Hargrave and Henry Hargrave (page 21) dressed in fashionably formal clothes.

References if needed or wished:

1. George Fox, *A Collection of Many Select and Christian Epistles . . .* (London, 1698), Epistle 227 (1663), p. 199.
2. George Fox (ed. John L. Nickalls), "An Exhortation of George Fox to Friends in the Ministry" from Launceston Prison 1656 (London, 1952), p. 263.
3. Norman Penney, ed., *The Journal of George Fox* 1 (Cambridge, 1911), p. 286.
4. Margaret Fox, *A Brief Collection of Remarkable Passages and Occurrences Relating to . . . Margaret Fell . . . by her Second Marriage, Margaret Fox* (London, 1710), Library of the Religious Society of Friends, London.
5. Ms. letter of Margaret Fox to Friends, 2nd (month) 1700, Portfolio 25/66, Library of the Religious Society of Friends, London.
6. "An Apology for the Life of George Anne Bellamy, late of Covent-Garden Theatre. Written by Herself . . ." (1785) as quoted in *Journal of the Friends' Historical Society* 17 (London, 1920): p. 47.
7. *A Supplement to Rules of Discipline* (London, 1849), p. 378, Library of the Religious Society of Friends, London.
8. *Nehustan; A Letter Addressed to the Members of the Society of Friends on their Peculiarities of Dress and Language* (London, 1859), p. 12.
9. Minutes of London Yearly Meeting 1860, Library of the Religious Society of Friends, London.
10. George Fox, *A Collection of . . . Epistles* (London, 1698), Epistle 7 (1667), p. 300.
11. Traditional phrase.
12. Reginald Leslie Hine, *A Mirror for the Society of Friends . . .* (London, 1929), Footnote XXIX, p. 66.

N.B. A fuller account of the development of a distinctive form of Quaker dress is to be found in *Costume 19,* the journal of the Costume Society of Great Britain (1985).

Master Edward Wakefield Pim
Mrs. Edward Pim

(actual size)

On page 34 in the folio other Pim duplicates can be found as well as these two that were cut in 1838. Master Edward selected the whip and toy horse from Edouart's bag of props. He is wearing a dress which was common practice for young boys.

Mr. Philip M. Price
Mrs. Philip M. Price

(actual size)

The Prices are the last silhouettes Edouart pasted in this Quaker folio on page 150½. Their travels can be traced to New Harmony, Indiana where an intellectual style life was advocated. They were cut October 1845 in Philadelphia.

Introduction: The Silence is Broken

Reader, would'st thou know what true peace and quiet mean; would'st thou find a refuge from the noises and clamours of the multitude; would'st thou enjoy at once solitude and society; would'st thou possess the depth of thy own spirit in stillness, without being shut out from the consolatory faces of thy species; would'st thou be alone and yet accompanied; solitary, yet not desolate; singular, yet not without some to keep thee in countenance; a unit in aggregate; a simple in composite:—come with me into a Quaker's Meeting.

The Essays of Elia and the Last Essays of Elia, by Charles Lamb (London: Oxford University Press, 1820–1833), p. 1.

It was believed by the early Quaker that the shadow was nature's own picture. Anna Cox Brinton stated in her 1964 book *Quaker Profiles:* "Friends belonging to the first generation of Quakerism consistently refused to have their portraits drawn or painted, they preferred to be remembered by their deeds, preserved in their journals, the Meeting records, or prefixed to early Quaker publications. Gradually the testimonies against portraits relaxed, simple likenesses in profile especially shadow pictures came to countenances." It is not unusual to find early ancestral albums filled with Quaker kin, the Society's leaders, and other tokens of affection. Now we find more Quaker shadows have been preserved by Augustin Edouart in these silhouette cuttings that were taken during the second quarter of the nineteenth century in England and America.

A personal narrative of Edouart's early life is recorded in his own words and spelling in a letter written to Miss Catherine Hutton, of Leamington, England, in 1837. This letter is in the Mary Martin Collection at the Metropolitan Museum, bequeathed in 1938.

In compliance with your request I give you a short abstract of my life.—I was the sixteenth and last child of my family; born the 27th January 1788. at Dunkerque département du Nord, France, my christian names are Augustin, Amand, Constant, fidel, my parents from independance were ruined in the course of the French revolution—My mother died when I was 7 yrs. of age.—5 of my brothers paid their life in the service of their country—When 15 yrs. of age being left with an unmarried sister to take care of our father who was paralettic, I began at that age to provide for myself:—at 19 I was director of a China manufactory at St. Iriex la Perche [where kaolin was discovered in 1765], in the south of France, having 120 workmen under my direction, where I remained about 2 yrs. when I returned to Paris and obtained a commission as Inspecteur des Fourages in Holland; from thence went into Germany where I had several services to fulfill, and was attached to the suite of La grande Armée going to Russia; Illness prevented me and returned to Holland—I was in Bergen-op-zoom when the English who stormed it were defeated—By the requisitions I made in the country I was the means of support in Antwerp in the time of the Siege; it is in that place that my military career ended. Being brought up in the Revolution, and likewise all devoted to Napoleon, I would not give my adhesion to Louis 18th on which account I was compelled to expatriate and arrived in London the 1st of August 1814. From that time to the present I support myself by talents which I had never thought of in my time of prosperity.

Life was to be a continuous struggle for this energetic émigré in this new place of asylum.

In late 1814, a young French mademoiselle, Emilié Lawrence Vital, became his bride. During their eleven-year marriage she bore him five children. To support his family Edouart taught French and crafted "hair work" jewelry and pictorial remembrances. His wife's unexpected death occurred in 1825 and plunged him into a deep state of depression.

Edouart recounts the discovery of a new direction in this quote from a book he had printed in Cork in 1834 with a London title page that was dated 1835 and entitled: *A Treatise on Silhouette Likenesses; by Monsieur Edouart, Silhouettist to the French Royal Family, and patronised by His Royal Highness the Late Duke of Gloucester and the Principal Nobility of England, Scotland, and Ireland:*

It was in the latter end of 1825, (having had the misfortune to lose Madame Edouart a short time before) I was sitting one evening with some friends, who shewed me Likenesses in bust of the Father and Mother of the Family, which had been taken with a patent machine; at the first view I condemned them as being unlike, and after having compared them with the originals, I pointed out to the daughters, where the faults lay; but they persisted that they were perfect, and that nothing could be better; the father and mother said nothing, but the young ladies who had engaged their parents to sit for them, insisted that it was impossible to have them more correct, and challenged me do them as well. I remonstrated that my finding fault was not a reason that I could do better, and that I had never, even dreamed of taking Likenesses; certainly to find fault with any object of art, or anything, was not to say that one could do the like; ladies when contradicted know how to revenge themselves, and the evening passed with sarcastic remarks, applied to my judgment, such as these, "criticism is easy and art difficult;" "Oh! it is not like at all!" and so on, 'till at last they upbraided me so much, (and my mind and spirits being so dull by my late misfortune,) I could not stand it any longer, and in a fit of moderate passion, I took a pair of scissors, that one of the young ladies used for her needle work; I tore the cover of a letter that lay on the table; I took the old Father by the arm and led him to a chair, that I placed in a proper manner, so as to see his profile, then, in an instant, I produced the Likeness; the paper being white, I took the black of the snuffers, and rubbed it on with my fingers: this Likeness and preparation, made so quickly, as if by inspiration was at once approved of, and found so like, that the ladies changed their teasing and ironical tone, to praises and begged me to take their Mother's Likeness, which I did with the same facility and exactness. They were so pleased at this extraordinary execution, that they asked to have theirs also, but in revenge I declined to do so.

These cuttings were the first by this Frenchman, who changed the name of the black shade to "silhouette." He is unexcelled in implementation of the shadow and surely the most prolific in this black art. For fourteen years he traveled England, Ireland, Scotland, and Wales, and, according to his own accounts, cut 50,000 silhouettes of superb quality preserving moments of stopped time.

We know that Edouart long contemplated a visit to America. He embarked on this desired journey at age fifty-one, leaving England in late March 1839 and arriving in the United States in mid-April. The exact day of arrival has never been established. Journals of the 1830s and 1840s noted that the duration of a voyage across the ocean lasted from fifteen to twenty-four days. His American career began in New York City, where he lodged with Roe Lockwood at 114 Broadway. For the next ten years he continued his art with talent, skill, and flexibility. This man who had been patronized by the royalty and nobility of Great Britain, was now the silhouettist to the elite of America. Edouart's reputation as an outstanding silhouettist preceded him to America and the reverential public was eager to engage his services at each place he traveled. One can follow his journeys by the ads he placed in the local newspapers announcing his impending arrival or departure.

His crisp delineations provide an authentic social picture gallery of prominent citizens, statesmen, six United States presidents (John Quincy Adams, Martin Van Buren, William Henry Harrison, John Tyler, Millard Fillmore, and Franklin Pierce), members of Congress, the military, journalists, men of letters, actors, bankers, members of the Society of Friends, their wives and children, each named and dated. He graphically depicted the most versatile and locally influential people with proficiency.

He toured the large population centers, spas, and resorts in the East, Midwest, North, and South, setting up studios to cut likenesses. His stays varied with the demand, but the volume of silhouettes he cut was great. After only five years in the United States, Edouart placed the following advertisement in the March 21, 1844, issue of the New Orleans newspaper, the *Daily Picayune:*

> Monsieur Edouart in presenting his grateful thanks to the inhabitants and visitors of the City of New Orleans for their liberal patronage, informs them that having to visit the towns on the Mississippi, he will close his establishment on the 25th. instant; he will be happy to continue to take likenesses or family groups till his departure, and his Exhibition of works of Art, with his extensive collection of 150,000 likenesses taken by him in Europe and the United States, will open (gratis) till that time, corner of Royal and Conti Street, opposite Louisiana Bank.

In 1849, with the help of his son, Edouart packed his English and American reference folios in cases for the return home on the sailing ship *Oneida*. The ship was laden with bales of cotton from Maryland, and a few passengers. Caught in a formidable storm off the rocky coast of the Isle of Guernsey, the ship wrecked in the Vazon Bay on December 21, 1849. The crew and passengers were saved and in the salvaged baggage were some of Edouart's duplicate folios, and a few of his lists, books, and letters; the rest was lost!

Monsieur Edouart was invited by Thomas Lukis, Esquire, of the Grange, Guernsey, to stay in his home while Edouart recovered from the trauma.

Edouart did not stay many days as his mind was in a continuous state of anxiety and when he departed he gave the Lukis family many of his recovered folios as a gift for their care and attention. He was devastated and could not bear to look at the meager remains of his life's work. The following quote was found in Mrs. F. Nevill Jackson, *Ancestors in Silhouette, Cut by August Edouart:*

> Of the Folios, saved, many seem to have been quite untouched by sea water, and the bindings, clasps, etc., are in perfect condition, though worn as one would expect them to be after such long use for exhibition. Edouart himself seems surprised at the small damage done.
>
> In a letter addressed to Thomas Lukis, Esq., Island of Guernsey, dated Calais, May 29, 1850, Edouart writes:—
>
> Calais, 29th May, 1850.
> Dear Sir,
> If I was not able to appreciate your good heart and likewise the humanly conduct of your family, towards a fellow creature in distress, I would be very unwelcome after 6 months silence to thank you for all your kind help at the time of my shipwreck.
>
> I wrote to Mr. Hry. Tupper on the 2nd April last and begged him to inform you of the reasons which occasioned my long Silence and said I would write to you in a short time to your dear family, but the season having been so bad that I got cold upon colds, and illness prevented me to accomplish my desire.
>
> Now that my mind and health are better, I take this opportunity to inquire about my Guernesey friends and at the same time to assure you all my true gratitude for what you have done for me.
>
> By the few things I took with me at my departure, I perceived that those who were damaged by sea water would not have been intirely lost, and if I had stopped a few days longer I could have carried more books and other objects with me. But the fear I was put in, that any thing touched by sea water would always be Damp prevented me to do so.
>
> I hope that your labor has been rewarded in saving many goods and books and other objects left at the farmer of Mr. _____. I forgot the name.
>
> As it would hurt my feelings to see them, I beg you dear sir, to act as if it was for yourself, if you can sell some to your friends or acquaintances do, and let me know of it, be carefull to keep the books I presented to your family, Mr. Tupper, and the Clergyman.
>
> I left several articles at the farm such as Paking cases, 2 large Tin boxes for books great number of frames, etc. etc. You may arrange all, that those good people may be satisfied and be so kind as to thank them for me for their good behavior towards my misfortune.
>
> At all events my dear Sir, what ever you have done and will do for me will be considered as a continuation of your kindness and never be forgotten.
>
> I am fearfull that I shall never intirely recover of the effects that the shipwreck has produced upon my mind and health.
>
> I do not know if Mr. Hry. Tupper has received my remittance.
>
> I am going to pass about 6 weeks in the country, if you favor me by your answer? will you be so kind as to direct to the care of Mr. Isaac Olivier my relation who will, if by chance you travel through Calais give you my residence.
>
> I beg you to presente my respects to your family and likewise to the families whom have been so kind to me, and believe me,
> Dear Sir,
> Your obedient and very
> humble servant,

He died at Quines near Calais in 1861 at the age of seventy-two. No evidence has been found that he resumed his career as a silhouettist after the accident.

To date there have been twenty-one duplicate folios recovered. Nineteen are still in existence; two mentioned in a letter in 1969 were lost in World War II. Mr. Andrew W. Tuer, a pioneer British critic, used Edouart's silhouettes to illustrate an article "The Art of Silhouetting" in the *English Pictorial Magazine* of the 1890s, which may have been responsible for the search for the lost folios.

Mrs. E. Nevill Jackson (E. or Emily used after her husband's death and F. Nevill before), a collector-writer-authority on silhouettes, placed a query in a 1910 issue of the *Connoisseur* magazine requesting the owners of old silhouettes to let her examine them for her research on the subject. She received a reply from the Lukis family of Guernsey in 1911 and the discovery began. She purchased fifteen folios from the family at that time and another in 1913. In 1921, Mrs. Jackson wrote a book entitled *Ancestors in Silhouette, Cut by August Edouart* in which she gave a complete description of the purchased folios. In 1978, Sue McKechnie authored *British Silhouette Artists and Their Work, 1760–1860,* a study that brings the Edouart English reference folios into even better focus. This newly identified Quaker book concentrates on both English and American cuttings of Edouart during the period 1827–1845.

The American folios (six of the sixteen purchased by Mrs. Jackson) were sold to Mr. Arthur S. Vernay, of New York, who marketed them in a three-week sale in America. He removed the silhouettes individually from the duplicate books and matted and framed them for the exhibition and sale. Interested descendants formed long lines to retrieve silhouettes of lost ancestors for preservation in family archives. The remaining 862 unsold silhouettes were sold in bulk to the Reverend Glenn Tilley Morse, of New England, a silhouette collector and writer. They remained in his collection until his death in 1950, when in accordance with Mr. Morse's will they became a part of the collection at the Metropolitan Museum of Art in New York City.

After Mrs. Jackson photographed and indexed the albums, she gave some to museums in Great Britain and Canada. The others remained in her possession until her death on February 7, 1947. Her silhouette collection and the remaining English albums were then divided between her son, the late Bernard Jackson, in America, and her daughter, the late Mrs. Betty Howard, at Mayfield, Sussex. The silhouettes given to Mr. Jackson still remain in his family. The collection in Mrs. Howard's possession were dispersed before her death in 1985.

The cover of the duplicate folio is Spanish-veined marbleized paper with red morocco leather corners, a brass catch (parts missing) and measures 14½" × 10½". The spine is now reinforced with library tape. Water damage is evident throughout.

The significance of finding another folio warrants close attention to the number of duplicate books in existence today:

Chronology of Duplicate Folio Rediscoveries

1911	Mrs. F. Nevill Jackson acquired 15 duplicate folios from the Fredrica Lukis family.	9 English / 6 American
1913	Mrs. F. Nevill Jackson acquired 1 additional folio from the Lukis family.	1 English
1930	Mrs. E. Nevill Jackson acquired from an unknown source a folio of genre silhouettes used for display in Edouart's studio.	1 genre folio
1977	E. F. Bonaventure, Inc., recorded an album on Feb. 3, 1923, and sold it to Miss Sarah C. Hewitt with 536 silhouettes. It sold at the Norvin H. Green sale on October 15, 1955, to John Shapiro, of Baltimore. Mr Shapiro sold it to a private collector in the 1970s. This private collector gave it to the National Portrait Gallery in Washington, D.C., in 1977 on indefinite loan, at that time containing 348 silhouettes with lithographed backgrunds and autographs of the sitters. This volume has been disassembled for permanent display. The entire folio was published (Andrew Oliver, *Auguste Edouart's Silhouettes of Eminent Americans, 1839–1844* [Charlottesville, Virginia, 1977]).	1 American
1983	The Friends Historical Library, of Swarthmore College, bought in 1969 from Mr. C. A. Defline, of France, a folio in November, containing Quaker profiles. artist was identified by Helen and Nel Laughon, silhouettists-researchers-collectors, October 24, 1983.	1 folio with English and Americans
	The 2 albums lost in the war—mentioned by Mr. Defline	2
	Total duplicate folios now identified	21

On October 24, 1983, Helen and Nel Laughon visited the Friends Historical Library, of Swarthmore College, at Swarthmore, Pennsylvania, to study silhouettes. After noting their keen interest in the Thomas Gilpin album and other silhouettes in the collection, the librarian emerged with a large folio of engaging full-length silhouettes. It was explained that the library had acquired the folio because of the quality and charm of the named and dated silhouettes of prominent families and individuals, who were members of the Religious Society of Friends; but the librarians were unaware of the creator's identity or style. They had received a letter from Mr. C. A. Defline, of France, on November 10, 1969. He had been advised to write to them concerning the silhouettes by the Friends' Library, Friends House, London, England. The letter follows:

> I don't know who was the artist, around 1840 who made the silhouettes, but I know that he was attached to the family of the wife of my father's uncle. She was English woman, named Moore, who married . . . Delsart (a lawyer in the town of Calais, northwest of France). This uncle had his home destroyed during the first war, and after his death, my father received three books of silhouettes, and a stamp collection. During the second war we lived in Amiens where our home was bombed and partly destroyed. This book was the only one saved and that is the explanation of the dampness.

The Laughons recognized the practiced hand of Augustin Amant Constant Fidèle Edouart (1789–1861). As they leafed gently through the pages, the realization that another folio had surfaced was overwhelming. The fact that it had survived the shipwreck was a researcher's dream. If the silhouettes had not been cut from the best quality of handmade paper, they would not have endured the circumstances that time had imposed. Only Edouart was the master of such delicate elements and careful record keeping. This folio has the rare distinction of being the only "American" duplicate album still intact, glued and bound in the original form.

The Quaker book measures 14½″ x 10½″, bound with Spanish-veined marbleized boards and a leather spine, reinforced with library tape and leather corners, which are worn. There is water damage on the pages and some silhouettes are missing because the glue dissolved in the water. The brass latch is broken, the title page lost, and several pages are loose from the binding.

On the cover tissue is a single, hand-inscribed word, "Friends." The ink from the lost title page had faded onto this tissue divider. After studying the information written below the feet of the numerous shadows, we transcribed it. Because of the variations of handwriting we found it difficult to decipher the inscriptions of names; dates; statistics of birth, death, marriage, and height; place of residence; and location of the cutting. Edouart usually wrote the information in his own hand, but at times he asked the sitters to add their personal signatures and details. The wide variety of information gives the album an unquestioned value as a socio-historical document.

As was the style of the 1830s and 1840s, a young lady who had married was referred to as "the late Miss" and a widow as "relict." Dates were written in the Continental manner with the day, month, and year contrary to the American sequence of month, day, and year. Fourteen of the sitters lack the annotation of place and date of cutting while only one is unidentified completely. In *A Treatise on Silhouette Likeness*, the artist states, "It has been my invariable practice to ask the names of my sitters, and write them on the backs of the duplicate, which duplicate I place in my book."

Sarah Fisher, seated, has Edouart's sketching and Miss Annie W. Fisher has pencil embellishments.

After 1842 Edouart consistently added white and pencil touches to the silhouettes.

Photograph by James McCann

Edouart further explained in his 1835 *Treatise* that his practice was to take a piece of paper, white on one side and black on the other, fold the black side in and sketch his subjects' profile in pencil on the white side, then cut it out obviously in duplicate. The extra cutting was saved in his albums much as a photographer saves negatives, to provide a reference for future cutting and advertisement. The silhouette given to the customer was mounted with gum arabic onto a background that was plain, lithographed, or watercolored and often placed in a flat curly maple frame with a gold liner.

Rather than attempting the time-consuming task of biographical and genealogical studies of each shadow, we have limited ourselves to presenting the silhouettes as art and a research tool.

For students of Edouart, this duplicate album affords the opportunity to study much of his career as a silhouettist in one folio. The subtle changes made in his style become visible to the eye. In the shades cut before 1842 he produced the plain black outline *only* as was his preference. It is well to note that Edouart began in 1842 to add embellishments of pencil and chalk, forced by the advent of the daguerreotype. This created a photographic appearance to the costumes, hair, and props. Delineation is found on 276 figures that date from 1842 to 1845. No matter how good his artistic additions, he found that people quickly followed the "new style" and put an end to yesterday's taste with photography's encroachment. Edouart's advertisement in the December 4, 1845, *Charleston Courier*, Charleston, South Carolina, reflects these changes:

> COLORED MINIATURE DAGUERREOTYPE LIKENESSES, Monsieur Edouart, From Paris, patronized by the Royal Families of France, England, the Presidents, and the most distinguished characters of the United States, beg to inform the inhabitants of this city and his friends, who have visited his fashionable Lounge at Saratoga Springs, that he has opened his GALLERY OF SILHOUETTES AND MINIATURE DAGUERREOTYPE LIKENESSES, where he will be happy to receive visitors and take likenesses in a style never before seen in Charleston, and approved by the first artists, who give him the most flattering praise for his perfection in the expression, attitude and coloring.
>
> Mr. E.'s collection of Physiognomies, in which he has represented himself in the degrees of different passions and characters, has already attracted the attention of the scientific personages of this city for their faithfulness to nature and spirit that those expressions and passions operate on the features of the human face.
>
> A visit to his Fashionable Lounge will give proof of his inimitable talent, and give him the satisfaction that the execution of his Likeness will receive the patronage that his work deserves.

Edouart now contradicts his own earlier statement in the *Treatise* demanding that the silhouette be entirely black!

The duplicates, while studied for individuality, offer a unique pattern of consistency that is familiar in all of his work. His "military standard" of 7½" to 8" is strictly adhered to for the figure size. Edouart's genius, joy of perception, and versatility are everywhere evident in the details in the costumes and furniture, elevating them above the surface of common things. His unwritten signature appears in the familiar slit collars backed with white paper, the delicate buttonholes, recurring hand positions, and pointed feet.

The members of the Society of Friends are captured in activities of daily living with ladies rocking, knitting, and congregating with their families and friends around the tea table. The personality of the men is reflected in their reading maps, conversing, and holding umbrellas, hats, books, watches, eyeglasses, and snuff boxes. Children are engagingly active playing badminton, or with their hoops and sticks, jump ropes, and pull horses. Tiny babies are waiting patiently on tasseled pillows or in loving arms. One small girl is sporting a crutch and a dog is waiting to shake the hand of his owner. Dolls, flowers, and even a silhouette cutter add to the "life" breathed into these pages. Edouart had the natural ability to think in the silhouette medium. He took artistic liberties and often placed additional pre-printed props of sheet music, scrolls, newspapers, maps, and letters in the paper figures' hands.

The folio explodes with the most minute hand-cut details: eighty-nine pieces of seat furniture, twenty tables with accessories, footstools, birds, books, pencils, a baby rattle, bows and arrows, tea services, baskets, stick horses, hats, fans, vases of flowers, gloves, bonnets, a potted plant, cups and saucers, a toy boat, silhouette and scissors, a riding whip, a quill pen, monocles, and pocketbooks.

There are twenty silhouettes taken by description or posthumously. Edouart describes his process:

> From description merely I have taken a great number of Likenesses, as also from single busts made by patent machines or by shadows on the wall. To those I have added the figure according to the description given me. I have taken others by other Likenesses pointed out in my books, as nearly resembling the likeness desired; and then by directions given at the time, I made, the requisite alterations til the Likeness was perfect. Every Likeness I have done in this manner has given entire satisfaction.

He once remarked that he wished people would have their shadows taken before death. He disliked working around a corpse, as it could be detrimental to his own health. Mr. Joshua Barker is one subject taken after death (page 136). His shadow was taken February 7, 1843, after he had died the previous day. The back of his head and legs are rigidly cut and not as well formed as is usual for the scissor artistry of Edouart representing this macabre note. Mr. Barker's sister Martha Hilles is pictured on the same page and taken the same day.

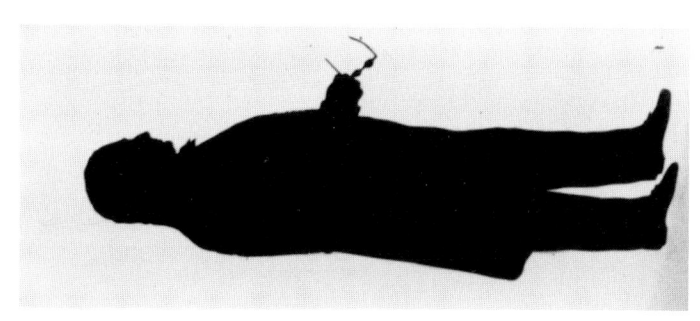

Joshua Barker at "rest" taken before his burial. (Cover the lower half of the body to see the subject as did Edouart).

The silhouette duplicates are mounted haphazardly as if reflecting their spiritual well-being in a Friend's popcorn (where several stand and speak) meeting. Sometimes pieces of a figure were cut separately and reapplied to change the position or make an alteration requested by the sitter. The back of the chair has been separated from Mrs. Robeson Lea (page 170). She also appears to have had the subtle effect of a few pounds snipped away. Richard Ball, Esquire (page 4), is shown in three poses. He must have been enamored with the process and the results, seeking to see himself in bust, full-length with glasses in hand, and then with stick and hat! Dr. Joseph Ball (page 4) also sought several renderings, one bust and one full with book and glasses. Edouart seemed pleased to accommodate the whims of his sitters. Copies of all the silhouettes were kept, but a final composition was rendered solely for the customer.

The entire folio format contains 782 Quaker sitters: 571 are still glued in place and 211 are missing but the identification remains. There are 138 Britons, 609 Americans, and busts of 35 Quaker luminaries. The sitters are recorded in full length with the exception of 46 busts and 1 three-quarter bust.

The 138 silhouettes of Britons are glued to pages 1 through 39. The earliest is of Benjamin Wilmore, 14 Gravel Lane, Blackfriar, London, taken October 6, 1827, in Cheltenham. The last British Quaker was

Edouart often gave lithographed copies of his self-portrait to special sitters. He included his autograph and a personal message.

*John Pim, cut in Belfast, March 23, 1839. Two American silhouettes glued in the British section out of time and place are *Miss Rachel Grellet and *Stephen Grellet, taken November 20, 1843, in Burlington, New Jersey.

The listing of places where Edouart performed his art for members of the Society of Friends include the following cities of Great Britain: Belfast; Birmingham; Bristol; Burlington; Cambridge; Cheltenham; Dublin; Edinburgh; Elmsfield City Down; Limerick; London; Mayallon, Ireland; Tewkesbury; Whitehaven; and Worcester.

Joseph Pease, Esquire, woolen manufacturer and banker; Richard Reynolds, iron producer; Stanley Pumphrey, Esquire, glove manufacturer; Nathaniel Hartland, banker; John Allis Hartland, Esquire, banker; John Pim Jackson, architect; and Lucy Clarke, silhouettist, are but few of the commissioned profiles contained in these pages that date from 1827 to 1839.

Pages 40 through 175 contain American cuttings from 1839 to 1845. There are 253 men, 220 women, 67 children, a dog, and a cat. The United States tour included: Baltimore; Boston; Burlington, New Jersey; Long Island; Mobile; New York; Philadelphia; Saratoga; Saratoga Springs; Shrewsbury, New Jersey; Washington, D.C.; and West Erie, Pennsylvania.

More than three hundred fifty silhouettes were cut in Philadelphia. Edouart's records mention familiar areas: streets—Arch, Chestnut, Locust, and Walnut; homes—Robeson Mill, Barclay Hall, Stenton, Kimberton, and Millverton; surrounding communities—Germantown, Chester County, and Bucks County.

Thomas Beaven Metford, Jr. (shadow missing), was taken in New York on April 15, 1839, and his is the earliest-recorded duplicate cutting by Edouart in this country and more accurately dates Edouart's arrival in the United States. The last Quaker silhouettes, of Mr. and Mrs. Philip Price, were cut in Philadelphia on October 14, 1845. The Quaker folio ends at this date, but the career of the French artist continued in the United States until 1849.

Edouart's fervent interest in his sitters is emphasized by the newspaper articles and personal notations glued throughout the book. Above the spot where Thomas Beaven Metford's silhouette was mounted is an article dated July 4, 1844, five years after his silhouette was taken: "Drowned while bathing, Samuel and Thomas Metford, age respectively 26 and 28 years and members of the Society of Friends were bathing yesterday off Fort Hamilton, L.I., and unfortunately went out over their depth, and before assistance could be rendered them, were drowned. We understand that they were natives of Bristol, England. Their bodies were recovered, and will be interred this afternoon."

There are profiles of doctors, lawyers, teachers, ministers of the gospel, abolitionists, government officials, and their families: Charles Perry, cashier of the Washington Bank; John T. Lewis, secretary of the Pennsylvania Hospital; Mordecai Lewis and Samuel Coates, managers of the Pennsylvania Hospital; Samuel Black, teacher; J. P. Lippincott, bookseller; Elwood Harvey, medical student; Gertrude Kimber, abolitionist; Elias Hicks, leader of the Hicksite Orthodox Separation movement; John Coates, lawyer for the estate of William Penn; Thomas Allan, doctor in Bucks County; M. L. Dawson, director of public schools and manager of Friends Asylum of Insane and of the Colony Institute; *Thomas Cope, developer in Philadelphia; Eli Price, lawyer; family members of the founders of the Wharton School of Business: *Charles, Rodman, William, *William, Jr., and Deborah F. Wharton; Charles Massey, warden of Philadelphia; Dr. Joseph Parrish, surgeon at the Pennsylvania Hospital; and Thomas Gilpin, silhouettist and author of *Exiles in Virginia: With Observations on the Conduct of the Society of Friends During the Revolutionary War . . .* (Philadelphia, 1848).

Several silhouettes invite special attention: Two slightly different outlines appear of Charlotte Temple Knowles, a black, whose silhouette was cut in New York City on October 21, 1839 (pages 50 and 50½). Inscribed under her figure with teacup in hand is the information that her father was born a slave in Martinique and that she was liberated at age five and was the servant of Mrs. Cooledge. Edouart thought blacks had characteristic features that were a challenge to cut according to his *Treatise*.

There are two groups designated as "Four Generations": (page 58) Mrs. Patience Corlies (great-grandmother), Mrs. Dobel Baker (grandmother), Mrs. Thomas Leggett (mother), and Anne T. Leggett (daughter); (page 61) Mrs. Hannah Hawxhurst (great-grandmother), Mrs. Sarah H. Marshall (grandmother), Mrs. William T. Moore (mother), and Infant Moore (grandchild).

Edouart identifies Mr. Julius Brainard (page 44½) and Mr. Leonard Hotaling (shadow missing page 45) with the written words "no friend," signifying that they were not Quakers. On the backs of others of the partially glued silhouettes appear the written verification that the sitter was a "Friend."

The group of folio pages, 176 through 203, are blank. A separate section, pages 204 through 206, contain 35 early members of the Religious Society of Friends. Sixteen of the missing silhouettes are noted by * before the name: (page 204) Thomas Scattergood, *Dr. John Wakley Lettson, William Rawle; (page 204½) *Samuel Shoemaker, Richard Smith, William Willson, Thomas Harrison, Daniel Williams, James Naylor, Robert Proud, *Samuel Coates, *Joshua Howell, Owen Jones, Dr. J. D. Griffiths, John Head; (page 205) Sarah Rhoads, *Mary Ridgway, George Delwyn (Dilwyn), Rebecca Jones, *John Pemberton, *Nicholas Waln, John Joseph Gurney, William Savery, Thomas Shillitoe, *James Pemberton, *Daniel Wheeler; (page 206) John Drinker, Josiah Hewes, *Mary Pleasant, *Richard Smith, *Thomas Paschall, *Samuel Pleasant, *Isaac Zane, *John Field, and *George Warner. Most are cut-and-paste copies by Edouart of inked-bust silhouettes originally painted by Joseph Sansom, Thomas Gilpin, and several unknown artists. If a request was made for a likeness of one of the leaders of the Society, it could be quickly provided to be used in a family album.

Many of these albums survive: the Joseph Sansom inked silhouettes at the Historical Society of Pennsylvania; two Canby family albums recently acquired by the Abby Aldrich Rockefeller Folk Art Collection in Williamsburg, Virginia (cut-and-paste, hollow-cut, and inked silhouettes); an unknown Quaker family's album of busts (cut-and-paste, inked, hollow-cut, lithographed silhouettes and a striking), and the Thomas Gilpin album (inked, hollow-cut, and lithographed silhouettes) at the Friends Historical Library, of Swarthmore College in Swarthmore, Pennsylvania; the Vaux family album in the collection of George Vaux, of Bryn Mawr, Pennsylvania (lithographs, striking, hollow-cut, and inked). The cut-and-paste copies in the Vaux album of Thomas Shillitoe and Daniel Williams are examples of this service Edouart offered from the Quaker Duplicate Book. This is by no means a complete list of the Quaker family albums that must exist.

In the Gilpin album is a special lithographed self-portrait silhouette of Augustin Edouart inscribed: "Presented to Thomas Gilpin, Esquire by his affectionate friend, Aug. Edouart, Philadelphia 1st March, 1843." Edouart cut Thomas Gilpin's seated silhouette on February 20, 1843, in Philadelphia (page 140) and added pencil details to the shadow.

Edouart had a classical-style, engraved silhouette self-portrait that he often gave to friends and sitters. In a letter he wrote: "I beg you Madame to receive my most sincere thanks for the honour confered on me and here take the liberty of subjoining my silhouette likeness."

There are many Quaker family albums. Two Canby family albums are in the Abby Aldrich Rockefeller Folk Art Collection.

Four titles for other duplicate books were referred to in this Quaker book, indicating that copies of some sitters were also in other folios. This is true of Benjamin Willmore, Dr. Samuel Morton, John C. Cresson, and Dr. Joseph Parrish, who are also listed in indexes compiled by Mrs. E. Nevill Jackson, Arthur S. Vernay, and Andrew Oliver. Morton, Cresson, and Parrish are included in a folio Edouart entitled "The American Character Book." This is the first reference noted in which Edouart gives a title to the book that is on permanent display at the National Portrait Gallery, Washington, D.C. The title given to the exhibit is "Eminent Americans." A reference is written beneath Mrs. Jane C. Fraley (page 158) concerning the fact that her husband is pictured on page 47½ of "The American Character Book." Edouart also makes reference to "The New York Book" (page 67½) by Miss Louisa Mott. Benjamin Willmore (page 1) was included in Mrs. Jackson's listings of the first nine English folios as having been taken on the same date and place as the one in the Quaker book. On the back of John Mayfield (page 1) is the penciled note that he could be found in the Cambridge and Eaton Folio #45.

Identification can now be ascribed to more nameless shadows on the wall. The Henry Francis DuPont Winterthur Museum, Inc., in Winterthur, Delaware, owns a family group known only as the work of Edouart, 1842. From the duplicates the names of Mrs. Hannah Hawxhurst, Mary Trimble, *Mrs. Daniel Trimble, Daniel Trimble, Mrs. William T. Moore and Infant Moore, and Mrs. Sarah Marshall, 264 East Broadway, New York, and the dates taken can be affixed to the composition (page 60).

Other original pictures with backgrounds that have duplicates in this folio have been located: Two Lea family groups (privately owned); the Vaux family (privately owned); the Underhills and Susanna Sansom family both pictured in *Quaker Profiles* by Anna Cox Brinton; the Dr. Joseph Cheesman and George Ring groups at the New-York Historical Society in New York City; and the Price family group (privately owned). When identification is sought the originals usually face in the opposite direction from the duplicates, since the paper was folded before cutting, making mirror images. The records that were kept in the duplicate books do not appear on the completed silhouettes. Edouart usually signed his name in ink in either corner, "Aug.ⁿ Edouart, fecit," with the date and place, but left the family unnamed. As years have passed the generations have lost verbal identification of the sitters.

This Quaker duplicate folio has survived to remind us graphically of a period of history, costumes, furniture, social activities, occupations, and family importance. It represents Edouart's view through his art of an important religious community in a collection that has photographic realism.

For a man to refrain even from good words, and to hold his peace, it is commendable; but for a multitude, it is great mastery . . . to go and seat yourself, for a quiet half hour, upon some undisputed corner of a bench, among the gentle Quakers! Their garb and stillness conjoined, present a uniformity, tranquil and herdlike—as in the pasture—"forty feeding like one."

The silence is broken! The "Inner Light" shines!

Mrs. Letitia L. Cresson

(actual size)

In May 1843, Mrs. Cresson was cut in a familiar pose, seated in her special chair with gout stool and fan. The duplicate is on page 159.

Elias E. King
Francis T. King
(actual size)

This school day theme is often repeated in Edouart's reference books. These gentlemen had their shadows taken in Baltimore in 1840 and can be seen on page 98.

Miss Jane Chapman
Mr. Joseph Cresson, Jr.
(actual size)

On May 16, 1843, Jane Chapman was posed with her brother-in-law in Philadelphia. They and other family members are shown on page 146½ and 155–159.

Advantages of Keeping Duplicates and Forming a Collection

At the commencement of my career as a Silhouettist, I was actuated by a sort of instinctive foresight, as far as regards the keeping of copies, and subsequent experience has fully proved, that I have been right, in adopting this resolution. It has been my invariable practice, to ask the names of my sitters, and write them on the backs of the duplicates, which duplicates I place in my books: since then, this collection has been rapidly increasing, and now amounts to much more than 50,000 Likenesses; among which are to be found the most eminent public characters, of the Nobility, the Church, the Military, and the Bar, from England, Scotland, and Ireland; and the probability is, that should my health and sight permit, in a few years this collection will contain double the number it does at present. Many persons have wondered at the trouble I have taken, in keeping copies of my works, not considering the advantage I shall ultimately derive from them; as it seems to them that those who had once had their Likenesses, would not require them again, and they cannot conceive the use of their Likenesses in a collection, as they would not be known but by their immediate friends, and indeed, it appears to them that they could be of little use to posterity. In a word they seem to think, that my labour is useless, but if they could know, what proofs I can bring forward, of the many duplicates, which have been required of those who have made such observations, they would not reason so mistakenly. They do not know what effects might be produced upon the feelings of their friends, if they could, or could not, procure the facsimile of their departed friend. Too many persons are impressed with the idea, that when deceased, nobody will lament the loss of their society.

—A.E.
Treatise, p. 107

Quaker Duplicate Book

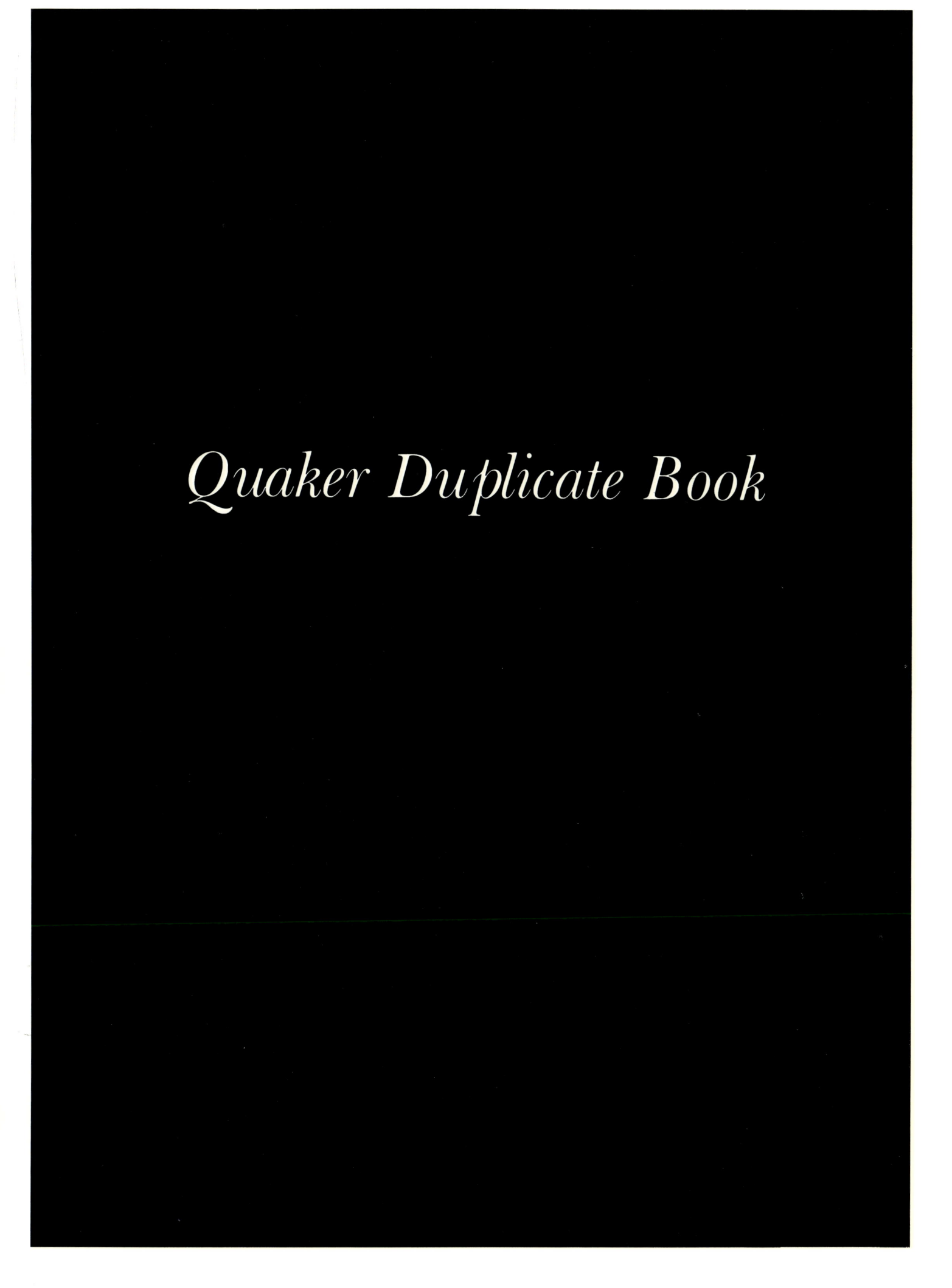

Sibbylla E. Price
Mary Ferris Price

(actual size)

Sibbylla and Mary prepared tea on a family tilt-top tea table. Notice Mary's crutch. The two girls were taken May 1843 in Philadelphia and their duplicates are on page 151.

The Album Records Include:

Name of sitter

Place of residence

Interesting notations

Date of cutting and place taken

EXAMPLE

P. 6

Miss Frances Lee

"Milverton"

(now Mrs. Edmund Burke Smith)

June 16, 1843—Philadelphia

The page numbers correspond to the Index of Sitters, page 109.
(All notations are as they appear in the duplicate album and are Edouart's spelling and arrangement).

Quaker Folio

Profiles taken in Great Britain
1827–1839

p. 1

* Edwards Harris	Theodore Waterhouse	Stanley Pumphrey, Esquire	John Mayfield of St. Ives	Benjamin Willmore
Royal Exchange	Royal Exchange	Worcester	(Eaton folio 45)	14 Gravel Lane, Blackfriar, London
October 6, 1828-London	October 7, 1828-London	November 25, 1829-Cheltenham	April 5, 1828-Cambridge	October 6, 1827-Cheltenham

* p. 1½

* Mrs. Amelia Opie	* Miss Rachel Grellet	* Stephen Grellet
of Norwich	3 Grenoble, N.Y.	3 Grenoble, N.Y.
June 20, 1828-London	November 20, 1843-Burlington	November 20, 1843-Burlington

p. 2

Henry Knight, Esquire	Miss Yerbury	Mrs. Holdship
June 29, 1829-Cheltenham	June 28, 1829-Cheltenham	Renter of the old spa (well)
		June 20, 1829-Cheltenham

*Silhouette missing

Quaker Folio

Miss Anne Farrer	**Joseph Pease, Esquire**	**Miss Pease**	**Joseph Pease, Esquire**
November 3, 1829-Cheltenham	Darlington Feethams	October 28, 1829-Cheltenham	October 28, 1829-Cheltenham
	October 28, 1829-Cheltenham		

p. 3

Richard Ball, Esquire, Obt. 1832
Foley Cottage, Red Land
October 5, 1829-Cheltenham

Dr. Joseph Ball
Bristol
October 1, 1829-Cheltenham

Mrs. Hannah Reynolds

Richard Ball, Esquire, Obt. 1832   **Richard Ball, Esquire,** Obt. 1832   **Dr. Joseph Ball**   **Richard Reynolds**
Foley Cottage, Red Land   Foley Cottage, Red Land   Bristol   Bristol-Obt. Sept. 10, 1816
October 5, 1829-Cheltenham   October 5, 1829-Cheltenham   October 1, 1829-Cheltenham Taken from a bust
                                                                                                                    October 1, 1829-Cheltenham

p. 4

*Silhouette missing

Quaker Folio

p. 5
Missing

p. 6
Missing

p. 7

Moses Goodere
November 24, 1829-Tewkesbury

Miss Goodere
November 24, 1829-Tewkesbury

Jacob Allis, Esquire
November 24, 1829-Tewkesbury

Jacob Allis, Esquire
November 24, 1829-Tewkesbury

p. 8

Nathaniel Hartland, Esquire
Obt. 1831, banker
November 24, 1829-Tewkesbury

Nathaniel Hartland, Esquire
Obt. 1831, banker
November 24, 1829-Tewkesbury

Rebecca Hartland
November 24, 1829-Tewkesbury

Alfred Harford Hartland
June 28, 1829-Cheltenham

John Allis Hartland, Esquire
banker
November 24, 1829-Tewkesbury

John Allis Hartland, Esquire
banker
November 24, 1829-Tewkesbury

John Allis Hartland, Esquire
banker
November 24, 1829-Tewkesbury

Anna Hartland, bust after death
November 24, 1829-Tewkesbury

Quaker Folio

p. 10

*Miss Graves	Miss W. Smith	Mr. William Spriggs	Mrs. William Spriggs
October 23–Edinburgh	Clapham Surrey	Worcester	March 14, 1837-Worcester
	October 2, 1830-Edinburgh		

p. 11

Miss Mary Robinson	Miss Hannah Mason	Thomas Simmons	John Todhunter, Esquire	Mr. William Robinson
February 4, 1833-Dublin	February 4, 1833-Dublin	age 83	85 Sir John Quai	9 College Green
		February 7, 1833-Dublin	January 19, 1833-Dublin	February 1, 1833-Dublin

Quaker Folio

Mrs. Richard Pim
February 16, 1833-Dublin

Miss Ruth Pim
February 16, 1833-Dublin

Mr. Richard Pim, Esquire
February 16, 1833-Dublin

p. 12

Mrs. Joseph Robinson
April 5, 1836-Limerick

Master M. Robinson
April 5, 1836-Limerick

Miss Eliza Robinson
April 5, 1836-Limerick

Mr. Joseph Robinson
April 5, 1836-Limerick

* **Mr. James Richardson**
April 14, 1836-Limerick

p. 13

*Silhouette missing

Quaker Folio

p. 14

John Pim, Esquire
London (family page 12)
February 16, 1833-Dublin

George Pim, Esquire
15 Usher Island
February 16, 1833-Dublin

Mr. Abraham Abel
Patrick Street-Cork
July 18, 1834

Edward Strangman
Waterford
July 14, 1836-Cheltenham

p. 15

Miss Isabella Nicholson Wakefield
July 20, 1836-Cheltenham

Elizabeth Wakefield
July 20, 1836-Cheltenham

Thomas Christy Wakefield, Esquire
Mogallton—Gilford City Down, Ireland
July 20, 1836-Cheltenham

Mrs. Jane Wakefield
7 Landsdown Place
Obt. July 10, 1836
July 1, 1836-Cheltenham

Quaker Folio

p. 16
Missing

p. 17
Missing

p. 18
Missing

p. 19

William Cooke	**William Bell Allen**	**John Pim Jackson**	* **Georgiana Eliza Jackson**	**Lucy Clarke**
of Ilchester	12 Talbot Street	architect	(born Oct. 22, 1835)—3' tall	silhouettist, Theslelugh Co.—Wicklow
April 4, 1838-Birmingham	December 13, 1838-Belfast	December 13, 1838-Belfast	Dec. 11, 1838-Belfast	March 13, 1839-Birmingham

p. 20

William Shorthouse, Esquire
taken by description,
Obt. June 10, 1838, age 69
July 10, 1838-Mosely, Birmingham

Mrs. William Shorthouse
July 13, 1838-Birmingham

Mrs. Fletcher Nicholson
daughter of Mr. & Mrs. William Shorthouse
July 18, 1838-Birmingham

*Silhouette missing

Quaker Folio

p. 21

* Mrs. William Hargrave	* Miss Caroline Hargrave	Miss Louisa Hargrave	Henry Hargrave	* Mr. William Hargrave
(daughter of Mr. & Mrs. William Shorthouse, page 20)	4' 4½" tall—age 13½	4' 6" tall—age 11 years 3 months	4' 1" tall—age 8½	London—taken by description Obt. November 10, 1832—age 47
July 2, 1838-Birmingham	July 2, 1838-Birmingham	July 2, 1838-Birmingham	July 2, 1838-Birmingham	July 2, 1838-Birmingham

p. 22

Mrs. Hannah Nutter	Mrs. William Nutter	Miss Amelia Nutter	Mr. William Nutter
taken by description Obt. March 25, 1837—age 74	(daughter of Mr. William Shorthouse, page 20)	3' 3" tall—age 4½,	
June 5, 1838-Birmingham	June 5, 1838-Birmingham	June 5, 1838-Birmingham	June 5, 1838-Birmingham

*Silhouette missing

Mrs. Sarah Smith
(mother to Hannah Nutter)

Mrs. William Nicholson
of Whitehaven

James Nicholson
(Obt. 1836 of Whitehaven—age 43)

Samuel Nutter
(Obt. July 17, 1831—age 34)

Benjamin Nutter
(Obt. 1831—Philadelphia, U.S.—age 32)

p. 22½a

Richard Burlingham
(died at St. Christopher, W.I.—age 24)
April, 1838-Evesham

p. 22½b

Quaker Folio

p. 23

Mr. Joseph Clarke	**Miss Ellen Clarke**	**Mrs. Joseph Clarke**	**Miss Sarah Clarke**
June 13, 1838-Birmingham	3' 4½" tall—age 5¼	(daughter of Mr. William Shorthouse, page 20)	(aunt to Mr. Joseph Clarke)
	June 13, 1838-Birmingham	June 13, 1838-Birmingham	June 13, 1838-Birmingham

p. 24

Miss Anna Marie Southall	**Miss Isabel Southall**	**Miss Ellen Southall**	**Miss Marguerite Southall**
June 20, 1838-Birmingham	3' 10" tall—age 6½	4' 5" tall—age 11½	4' 3" tall—age 10
	June 20, 1838-Birmingham	June 20, 1838-Birmingham	June 20, 1838-Birmingham

(All grandchildren of Mr. William Shorthouse, page 20)

Quaker Folio

* Samuel Dickinson	James Pearson, Esquire	Timothi Gill, Esquire
June 6, 1838-Birmingham	(head missing) July 8, 1838-Birmingham	London—taken by description (Obt. July 25, 1825—age 51) (uncle of Mr. William Nutter page 22) July 10, 1838-Birmingham

p. 25

* Miss Mary Bakewell	* Miss Rebecca Howell	* Mrs. Lucy Freeth	* Miss Lucy Freeth
Nottingham June 20, 1838-Birmingham	June 7, 1838-Birmingham	July 13, 1838-Birmingham	July 13, 1838-Birmingham

* p. 26

* William Man Shillitoe, Jr.	* Mrs. Thomas Shillitoe	Miss M. A. Shillitoe	* Mr. John Conran
May 5, 1838-Birmingham	Totterham, nr. London July 16, 1838-Birmingham	Union Street July 16, 1838-Birmingham	taken by bust and description (Obt. April 7, 1820) (born o:s Oct. 20, 1739)-Belfast

p. 27

*Silhouette missing

Quaker Folio

p. 28

| **Tobias Pim** | **Miss Hannah Pim** | **Mrs. Hannah Pim** |
| September 11, 1838-Belfast | September 11, 1838-Belfast | September 11, 1838-Belfast |

* p. 29   * **Mr. George C. Pim**   * **Mrs. George C. Pim**   * **Miss Mary Pim**   * **Mary Jane Phelps**
September 12, 1838-Belfast   September 12, 1838-Belfast   2' 4" tall—age 16 months   (sister of Mrs. George Pim)
September 12, 1838-Belfast   November 17, 1838-Belfast

p. 30

* **John Pim, Sr., Esquire**   * **Samuel Pim**   * **Marguerite Pim**   **Miss Mary Strangman Pim**
March 23, 1837-Belfast   April 20, 1837-Belfast   March 23, 1837-Belfast   (Obt. April 19, 1837—age 17 years 17 days)
Belfast

*Silhouette missing

Quaker Folio

p. 31

Mrs. Joseph Malcomson
Glen Mills-Guilford City Down
(daughter to Mrs. S. Greer)
September 19, 1838-Belfast

Mr. Joseph Malcomson
October 4, 1838-Belfast

Mrs. Samuel Greer (Jane)
September 26, 1838-Belfast

Miss Eliza Greer
September 26, 1838-Belfast

p. 32

Master William Henry Webb
2' 4" tall—age 15 months
November 13, 1838-Belfast

Wilhelmina Webb
age 7 years 3 months
November 13, 1838-Belfast

William Webb, Esquire
November 13, 1838-Belfast

Miss Charlotte Webb
3' 3" tall—age 6 years 1 month
November 13, 1838-Belfast

Mrs. Thomas Lamb
age 78, (mother to Mrs. William Webb)
September 19, 1838-Belfast

Quaker Folio

p. 32½

Mrs. Maria Webb	* **Anna Webb**	* **Miss Wilhelmina Webb**
November 13, 1838-Belfast	3′ 3″ tall—age 5 years, 7 months	3′ 2″ tall—age 7 years 3 months
	November 13, 1838-Belfast	November 13, 1838-Belfast

* p. 33

* **Mr. Joseph Barcroft**	* **Mrs. Samuel Alexander**	* **Miss Mary Bell**	* **Mrs. Joseph Barcroft**
Hangmore Lodge, Dungannon	(sister to Miss Mary Bell)	(aunt of Mrs. Joseph Barcroft)	(sister to John Wright page 52)
September 29, 1838-Belfast	October 4, 1838-Belfast	March 2, 1839-Belfast	March 2, 1839

p. 34

Miss Charlotte Dawson	**Master Edward Wakefield Pim**	**Mrs. Edward Pim**	**Edward Pim**
Elmsfield City Down	age 1 year 4 months	December 31, ——	October 2, 1838
September 12, 1838	October 11, 1838		

*Silhouette missing

Quaker Folio

* **Mrs. John Wakefield**	**Thomas Christy Wakefield**
December 20, 1838-Belfast	Mogalton, Guilford City Down
	July 20, 1836-Cheltenham

p. 34½

* **Mrs. John Wakefield**	* **Mrs. Mary Bell**	* **John B. Wakefield**
(daughter of Mrs. Mary Bell)	Greenmount, Ireland	Born Dec. 25, 1824
January 16, 1839-Belfast	January 16, 1839-Belfast	January 16, 1839-Belfast

* p. 35

p. 36

* **William Harvey**	**Miss Marguerite Harvey**	**Miss Marguerite Harvey**
(brother of Miss Marguerite Harvey)	October 5, 1838-Belfast	October 5, 1838-Belfast
November 26, 1838-Belfast		

p. 37 Missing

p. 38 Missing

p. 39 Blank

*Silhouette missing

Quaker Folio

Profiles taken in the United States
1839–1845

p. 40

* Mr. Shotwell, Sr.	Miss Anna H. Shotwell	Miss Mary Shotwell	* Mrs. Sarah Shotwell
Taken from bust and description	283 East Broadway	283 East Broadway	age 74, 283 East Broadway
October 14, 1839-New York	October 14, 1839-New York	October 14, 1839-New York	October 14, 1839-New York

p. 41

Mr. William Shotwell	Mrs. William Shotwell
187 Henry Street	187 Henry Street
February 17, 1840-New York	February 17, 1840-New York

*Silhouette missing

Quaker Folio

p. 42

| **Mr. George G. Haydock** | **Miss Hannah Wharton** | **Mary Haydock** | **Robert Haydock, Jr.** | * **Samuel Haydock, Sr.** |
| June 17, 1840 | (married Robert Haydock, Jan. 26, 1843 at 7 o'clock) October 6, 1842-Philadelphia | November 11, 1839-Philadelphia | October 12, 1839-Philadelphia | (Obt. April 18, 1842) October 12, 1839-Philadelphia |

p. 43

| * **Priscilla Barker** | **Wager Hull** |
| January 10, 1841-New York | October 10, 1839-New York |

*Silhouette missing

Quaker Folio

*p. 44

* **Jeremiah Brown**	* **Ed O. Brown**	* **Charles Brown**	* **Mrs. Jeremiah Brown**	* **John M. Brown**
107 Willow Street, Brooklyn			(daughter of Mrs. John Mabbett, page 45)	
February 25, 1840-New York				

p. 44½

Julius Brainard — (no Friend) (married Miss Mary Mabbett) May 18, 1840-New York

Sarah T. Mabbett

Ann H. Mabbett

Camilla E. McCarty (with cat)

*p. 45

* **Mrs. Julius Brainard**	* **Mr. Leonard G. Hotaling**	* **Mrs. Leonard G. Hotaling**	* **Elizabeth T. Mabbett**	* **Mr. John Mabbett**
(daughter of Mr. John Mabbett)	(no Friend)	(the late Miss Margaret H. Mabbett)	November 21, 1839	177 Grand, New York
	November 28, 1839	November 28, 1839		July 27, 1839-New York

p. 46

Joseph Lea, Jr. — 32 Chestnut Street, Philadelphia — October 29-New York

Joseph Lea, Sr. — "Milverton," near Philadelphia — November 22, 1839-New York

Mrs. Hanson Tucker-New Bedford (Miss Martha Robeson, niece of Joseph Lea) November 22, 1839-New York

Miss Catherine M. Lea — Philadelphia — November 22, 1839-New York

*Silhouette missing

Quaker Folio

p. 46½

Miss Caroline Justice
October 12, 1842-Philadelphia

p. 47

Miss Elizabeth Justice	**Mrs. George N. Justice (Esther)**	**Mr. George N. Justice**	**Rudolph Justice**	**George Justice**
October 11, 1842-Philadelphia	October 12, 1842-Philadelphia	October 11, 1842-Philadelphia	October 11, 1842-Philadelphia	October 11, 1842-Philadelphia

* **Elizabeth Yates**, (no. 2)	* **Thomas Beaven Metford, Jr.**, (no. 2)	* **Cornelia Metford**, (no. 2)	* **Daniel Cooledge**, (no. 2)	* **Joseph Metford, Sr.**, (no. 2)
November 4, 1839-New York	April 15, 1839-New York	(born Feb. 23, 1836) (daughter of Francis Metford, page 49) November 4, 1839-New York	November 4, 1839-New York	"Millbrook," Southampton, England November 4, 1839-New York

p. 48

	* **William J. Cooledge, Jr.**	* **Mrs. Daniel Cooledge**	* **Samuel Metford**	* **Francis Metford**
	October 25, 1839-New York	October 25, 1839-New York	Bath, England (drown July 4, 1844) left 5 years since October 25, 1839	Bath, England (arrived November 9, 1834) October 25, 1839-New York

*p. 49

*Silhouette missing

Quaker Folio

p. 50

Charlotte Temple Knowles
(Her father was a slave at Martinique)
(servant to Mrs. Cooledge)
liberated at 5 years
October 21, 1839

Miss Eleanor Metford
October 21, 1839-New York

Mrs. Francis Metford
(late Miss Phebe Cooledge)
October 21, 1839-New York

Mr. George Cooledge
374 Pearl Street
December 4, 1839-New York

* **Joseph Metford, Sr.,** (no. 2)
"Millbrook" Southampton, England
November 4, 1839-New York

p. 50½

Charlotte Temple Knowles
a slave
October 21, 1839-New York

Henry Metford
physician-London
(Obt. March 10, 1840—age 28)
Taken by description from bust

*Silhouette missing

Quaker Folio

p. 51
Blank

p. 52

James C. Bell	* **Abraham Bell**	* **John Wandesford Wright**	**William Bell**
October 22, 1839–New York	423 Broom Street, Broadway	(Abraham Bell's nephew–Belfast, Ireland)	(page 52½a, same child older)
	March 7, 1840–New York	(sister married Joseph Barcroft, page 38)	March 7, 1840–New York
		(his aunt, Mrs. Samuel Alexander, page 33)	

p. 52½a

William Bell
5'1" tall
December 11, 1844–New York

*Silhouette missing

Quaker Folio

p. 52½b

Miss Anne Eliza Bell, (no. 2)

p. 53

Miss Jane Jackson	**Miss Mary Bell**	* **Miss Rebecca Bell, (Mrs. Harvey)**	**Mr. Thomas C. Bell**	**Mrs. Thomas C. Bell** (late Miss Jackson)
Philadelphia	May 1, 1840-New York	May 1, 1840	Bayside Long Island	Bayside Long Island
(married May, 1840, Mr. Thomas C. Bell)			March 7, 1840	May 25, 1840
May 25, 1840-New York				

*Silhouette missing

Josiah G. Macy
June 17, 1840-New York

Joseph D. Thurston
June 6, 1840-New York

Isaac N. Wright
November 15, 1839-New York

Silvanus T. Jenkins
June 17, 1840-New York

p. 54

Richard Wright
(sister, page 33, brother, John, page 52)
January 24, 1843-Philadelphia

* **George A. Wright**
May 22, 1843-Philadelphia

John W. Wright
(Friend)—Belfast
October 23, 1839-New York

Samuel C. Morton
. Philadelphia
May 29, 1843-Belfast, Ireland

p. 55

*Silhouette missing

Quaker Folio

p. 56

Edward Hopper
of Philadelphia
September 24, 1842

Isaac T. Hopper
July 30, 1839-New York

John Hopper, Jr.
July 29, 1839-New York

p. 56½a

Isaac H. Brown
taken after his death
(grandson of Isaac T. Hopper page 56, 56½)
(born August 22, 1835—died December 30, 1839)

Isaac T. Hopper
July 30, 1839-New York

Dr. Josiah Hopper
November 17, 1843-New York

*p. 56½b

* **Christine Rabb**
from Germany
5′ 2″ tall—age 21 years 2 months
(18 months in America)
(Nurse to Samuel T. Gibbons family)

* **Lucy Gibbons**
2 months 6 days old (held by Miss Rabb)

* **Julia Gibbons,** (no. 2)
age 2 years 6 months

*Silhouette missing

Quaker Folio

* **James L. Gibbons**	* **William Gibbons**	* **Sarah Gibbons**	* **Mrs. Abigail H. Gibbons**
150 Eldridge Street	3' 9" tall (born Jan. 16, 1834)	3' 5" tall (born Sept. 19, 1835)	(late Miss Abigail Hopper)
January 3, 1840-New York	January 3, 1840-New York	January 3, 1840-New York	(her father, page 56)
			January 3, 1840-New York

*p. 57

Four Generations

p. 58

Mrs. Thomas Leggett [mother]	**Mrs. Patience Corlies** [great grandmother]	**Anne T. Leggett** [daughter]	**Mrs. Dobel Baker** [grandmother]
(late Patience Haydock)	age 89—(Died April 12, 1840)	November 11, 1839-New York	(daughter of Mrs. Corlies)
(father on page 42)	November 11, 1839-New York		November 11, 1839-New York
November 11, 1839-New York			

p. 58½

Miss Sarah H. Baker
November 11, 1839-New York

*Silhouette missing

Quaker Folio

p. 59

Mr. Walter T. Leggett
14 Henry Street, N.Y.
April 24, 1840-Philadelphia

Thomas Leggett, Jr.
New York
October 28, 1842-Philadelphia

George Corlies Baker
New York
April 24, 1843-Philadelphia

Mrs. Margaret G. Corlies
May 6, 1840

p. 60

Daniel Trimble
264 East Broadway
February 22, 1840-New York

Mary Trimble
(born August 3, 1829)
February 22, 1840

* **Mrs. Daniel Trimble**
February 22, 1840

*Silhouette missing

Quaker Folio

* **Miss Mary Trimble**
(born August 3, 1829)
February 22, 1840

* p. 60½

p. 61

Four Generations

Mrs. Sarah H. Marshall [grandmother]
(daughter of Mrs. Hannah Hawxhurst)
March 21, 1840-New York

Infant Moore [grandchild]
March 21, 1840-New York

Mrs. William T. Moore [mother]
March 21, 1840-New York

Mrs. Hannah Hawxhurst [great grandmother]
(mother of Mrs. Trimble, page 60)
March 21, 1840-New York

p. 62

Thomas Hawxhurst
age 88 years 1 month—died 1843
April 15, 1840-New York

Thomas Hawxhurst
age 88 years 1 month—died 1843
April 15, 1840-New York

*Silhouette missing

Quaker Folio

* p. 63

  * Charles V. Howland
  Union Springs, Cayuga County, New York
  November 9, 1842-Philadelphia

  * Mr. Mathew Howland
  New Bedford
  October 11, 1842-Philadelphia

  * Mrs. Mathew Howland
  New Bedford
  October 11, 1842-Philadelphia

p. 64

Robert White, Jr.	*** Phebe C. White**	*** Mr. Phinneas Janney**	*** Mrs. Phinneas Janney (Sarah S.)**	**Solomon Griften**
Shrewsbury, N.J.	March 2, 1840	born 1778, Alexandria, D.C.	born June, 1785	New York
January 14, 1840		September 9, 1844-Saratoga	September 9, 1844-Saratoga	August 10, 1844-Saratoga

p. 64½

Mrs. Sarah C. Hawxhurst	**Mr. Joseph B. Collins**	**B. S. Collins**	**Charles Collins** obt.
September 25, 1843-New York	November 14, 1843-New York	November 14, 1843-New York	October 25, 1843-New York

*Silhouette missing

Quaker Folio

Isaac Collins	Thomas Collins	Mrs. Stacy B. Collins	Mr. Stacy B. Collins	Mrs. Susanna R. Smith
November 1, 1843-Philadelphia	(Born March 3, 1779) June 1, 1843-Burlington, N.J.	(late Hannah W. Jenks) November 14, 1843-New York	November 14, 1843-New York	(Stacy Collin's sister) June 3, 1843-Burlington, N.J.

p. 65

John H. Andrews	* Sarah C. Rively	Rebecca Collins	Miss Hannah N. Collins	Hannah M. Neall
Darby Del. Co., Pennsylvania May 29, 1840-New York	Darby Del. Co., Pennsylvania (sister-in-law of John H. Andrews) May 29, 1840	(niece of Stacy B. Collins, page 65) July 20, 1841-New York	June 8, 1840-New York	Lynn, Mass. June 8, 1840-New York

p. 66

*Silhouette missing

Quaker Folio

p. 66½

* **Samuel T. Mott, Sr.**
July 16, 1845-Saratoga

Mrs. George Ring
(daughter of John Mott)
March 17, 1840-New York

p. 67

Samuel T. Mott, Jr.
March 25, 1840-New York

Samuel T. Mott, Sr.
262 E. Broadway
March 25, 1840-New York

Miss Louisa Mott
(married John J. Ring)
(see New York Book, page 144)
March 26, 1840

Ann Elizabeth Mott
262 E. Broadway
Born 1835—Obt. 1842
March 25, 1840-New York

Mr. Samuel T. Mott, Sr.
July 16, 1845-Saratoga

*Silhouette missing

Quaker Folio

* Miss Harriet S. Mott	* William T. Mott, Jr.	* Mablon Day	* Samuel C. Paxton	* p. 68
Long Island	March 4, 1840-New York	July 18, 1845-Saratoga	July 16, 1845-Saratoga	
April 2, 1840				

p. 68½

Mr. Samuel B. Parsons, Jr. **Mr. Samuel B. Parsons, Sr.** preacher **Samuel B. Parsons, Jr.**
October 18, 1842-Philadelphia March 30, 1840-Philadelphia May 30, 1840-Philadelphia

p. 69

Mr. James B. Parsons * **Elizabeth J. Parsons,** age 8 * **Mrs. James B. Parsons** * **John Brown Parsons,** age 6 * **Samuel Parsons, Sr.**
April 14, 1840-New York April 14, 1840-New York April 14, 1840-New York (obt. June 1845 by a fall from horse) obt. 1841
       April 14, 1840-New York April 14, 1840-New York

*Silhouette missing

Quaker Folio

*p. 70

* **Thomas Woodward, Jr.,** (no. 2)
February 28, 1840-New York

* **John D. Woodward**
(lost in the Erie Steamboat—August 1841 on Lake Erie)
February 28, 1840-New York

* **Thomas Woodward, Sr.,** (no. 1)
February 28, 1842-New York

p. 71

* **Mrs. Stephen Gaines,** (no. 1)
(widow Marther R. Griften)
(daughter of Mrs. Woodward)
1843

* **John Griften**

Mrs. Thomas Woodward, (no. 2)
186 East Broadway
(Obt. 1843)
February 28, 1840-New York

Miss Elizabeth Woodward, (no. 2)
186 East Broadway
February 28, 1840-New York

*p. 72

Benjamin Cox (Cock)
23 Clift Street
April 22, 1840-New York

Susan Cox
(widow of Abraham William Cox, Flushing)
April 21, 1840-New York

* **William Henry Cox**
April 21, 1840-New York

* **Jordon Wright**
April 21, 1840-New York

*Silhouette missing

Quaker Folio

* Alfred Smith	* Oscar Bloodgood Smith	Mrs. Alfred C. Smith	* Charles Cox (Cock)
Flushing	(infant)	(Mrs. Cox's daughter)	Flushing
April 29, 1840-New York	April 22, 1840-New York	April 22,1840-New York	April 22, 1840-New York

p. 73

* Elijah Cornell	Miss Cornell	Mrs. Elijah Cornell	Mrs. Sarah R. Lavender
31 Beckman Street	31 Beckman Street	31 Beckman Street	31 Beckman Street
April 23, 1840-New York	April 23, 1840-New York	April 23, 1840-New York	April 23, 1840-New York

p. 74

*Silhouette missing

Quaker Folio

p. 75

Maria W. O'Brien	Mr. William Binns	Mrs. William Binns
Buffalo County, Erie	31 Beckman Street	31 Beckman Street
October 13, 1840	April 23, 1840-New York	(daughter of Elijah Cornell, page 74)
		April 23, 1840-New York

p. 76

Mr. Abraham S. Underhill	Miss Anna Underhill	Miss Hannah Underhill, (no. 1)	Miss Sarah Underhill, (no. 2)
40 Market Street	40 Market Street	40 Market Street	40 Market Street
February 25, 1840-New York	February 25, 1840-New York	February 25, 1840-New York	February 25, 1840-New York

Quaker Folio

Alice L. Underhill
February 19, 1840-New York

* **Miss Elizabeth Underhill** (no. 2)
40 Market Street
February 19, 1840-New York

p. 76½

p. 77
Missing

p. 78
Missing

Mrs. Eunice Mitchell
(mother of Mrs. Walter Underhill)
February 14, 1840-New York

p. 78½

*Silhouette missing

Quaker Folio

*p. 79   * **Thomas Walker**   * **John B. Walker**   **Robert J. Walker**   * **Richard L. Walker**   **Robert Walker**   * **Mrs. Robert J. Walker**
4' 6" tall—born June 1828   died in Leeds, England   February 20, 1840-New York   3' tall—born August 28, 1838   born Jan. 21, 1834—3' 9" tall   (late Hannah Mitchell)
   June, 1845-New York   New York   February 20, 1840   (see her mother page 78½)
                         February 20, 1840-New York

p. 80

J. C. Cheesman, Jr.   * **Dr. J. C. Cheesman, M.D.**   * **Mrs. J. C. Cheesman**   **Miss Ann Cheesman**
473 Broadway, N.Y.   473 Broadway   473 Broadway, N.Y.   473 Broadway, N.Y.
March 20, 1840-New York   March 20, 1840-New York   March 20, 1840-New York   March 20, 1840-New York

p. 81

* **Mr. J. R. Willis**   * **Mrs. J. R. Willis**   * **Master Willis**   **Mrs. Elizabeth V. Willis**   * **Gilbert Congdon**   **Mr. Welcome Congdon**
August 12, 1841   August 12, 1841   August 12, 1841   (Late Miss E. V. Underhill, page 76½)   Providence, R.I.   Providence, R.I.
               August 12, 1841   November 12, 1842-Saratoga   November 17, 1842-Boston

*Silhouette missing

Quaker Folio

* Ellis Yarnall, Jr.	William S. Carpenter	Israel W. Tappan	* Sillas Clapp	* John Sholl
Philadelphia	March 19, 1840	February 13, 1840-Boston	March 11, 1840	born July 21, 1777
November 11, 1839-New York				(Pat. the Beehive barrel house from Spitalfield House, London)
				October 14, 1839-New York

p. 82

Henry H. Barrow	Master Henry Barrow	Samuel H. Clapp	Lawrence Waterbury	Stephens G. Hinsdale
March 31, 1840-New York	March 31, 1840-New York	109 Henry Street	March 14, 1840-New York	April 3, 1840-New York
		February 14, 1840		

p. 83

* Hugh H. Bowne	* Pennell Churchman	* Samuel L. Haight	* John Malcomson	* C. L. Halsted
New Jersey	October 29, 1839-New York	186 Chatham	of Belfast (Mobile)	April 18, 1840-New York
March 6, 1840-New Jersey		April 18, 1840-New York	November 2, 1839	

* p. 84

*Silhouette missing

Quaker Folio

p. 85

Miss Henrietta Hull
(married Mr. Cowdrey, March, 1841)
May 15, 1840-New York

Miss Rebecca Hull
May 15, 1840-New York

Mrs. Daniel D. T. Dibble
(widow, late Miss Ann Hull)
June 20, 1840-New York

* **Master Edward Dibble**
June 20, 1840

* **Rebecca F. Underhill**
(wife of Abraham of York Town,
West Chester Co.—page 76)
September 22, 1840-New York

p. 86

* **Mrs. Sarah S. Breed**
(68 years on the 16th inst., of Lynn, Mass.)
April 17, 1840-New York

Sarah S. Breed
Lynn, Mass.—W.a.h.
May 12, 1843-Philadelphia

* **Lucy J. Breed**
Jan. 21, 1843-Philadelphia (h.h.)

*Silhouette missing

Quaker Folio

William Jenkins	***P. H. Titus**	**Mrs. Benjamin Russell (Hannah)**	**Mrs. Peter Barney (Eliza)**	**Mr. James N. Buffum**
Providence, Rhode Island	New York	New Bedford, Mass.	(mother of Mrs. Benjamin Russell)	Lynn, Mass.
August 14, 1844-Saratoga	August 14, 1844-Saratoga	August 30, 1844-Saratoga Springs	August 31, 1844-Saratoga Springs	July 15, 1843-Saratoga Springs

p. 87

Miss Sarah D. Sharpless	**Anna Sharpless**	**Charles L. Sharpless**	**Henry H. G. Sharpless**	**Phebe Earle**
Philadelphia	June 9, 1840-New York	February 20, 1843-Philadelphia	June 9, 1840	Philadelphia
June 9, 1840-New York				September 18, 1839-New York

p. 88

*Silhouette missing

Quaker Folio

p. 88½

Miss Anna R. Williams
November 7, 1843-Philadelphia

p. 89

Miss Martha Leggett	**Aaron Leggett**	**Mr. Edward N. Wright**	**Miss Ann E. Harris**	**Hannah G. Watts**
(married Mr. Ben Cock)	(Martha Leggett's uncle)	Philadelphia	Philadelphia	August 14, 1841-Saratoga Springs
"Whitestone," Flushing, Long Island	"Whitestone," Flushing, Long Island	August 16, 1841-Saratoga Springs	August 16, 1841-Saratoga Springs	
May 10, 1840-New York	May 25, 1840-New York			

Quaker Folio

p. 90

* Phebe Anna Comstock	Miss Mary Smart
Washington, Dutchess County, New York	North Hartford near Utica, New York
May 27, 1840-New York	September 30, 1840-New York

p. 90½

Dr. Thomas Cock　　　　　　　　　　　　　　　　　　　Mrs. Thomas Cock

*Silhouette missing

Quaker Folio

p. 91

* **Dr. Thomas Cock, M.D.**	**Elizabeth R. Cock**	* **Mrs. Thomas Cock**
15 Murray Place	15 Murray Place—age 2½	May 10, 1840-New York
May 10, 1840-New York	May 10, 1840-New York	

p. 92

William R. Thruston, Jr.	**Charles Perry**	**Abel Francis Collins**	**Miss Elizabeth Perry**	**Thomas Perry**
May 26, 1840-New York	Westerly, Rhode Island	North Stonington, Conn.	(sister to Thomas Perry of Westerly, R.I.)	Westerly, R.I.
	(cashier of the Washington Bank)	May 29, 1840-New York	May 29, 1840-New York	May 29, 1840-New York
	October 27, 1840-New York			

*Silhouette missing

Quaker Folio

Samuel F. Cowdrey
October 16, 1840-New York

Josiah Howe
October 16, 1840-New York

John T. Lewis
Secretary of Pennsylvania Hospital
January 21, 1843-Philadelphia

Mordecai Lewis
Manager of Pennsylvania Hospital
November 3, 1842-Philadelphia

Otis Clapp
Wayne County
(head only, body missing)
March 20, 1841-Washington, D.C.

p. 93

Miss Isabella Johnson
(niece of Joseph Warner, page 173)
August 12, 1840-Philadelphia

Miss Martha Ann Johnson
(niece of Joseph Warner, page 173)
August 12, 1840-Philadelphia

Thomas Hopkins
Wey Hill, Talbot County, Maryland
September 7, 1844-Saratoga

p. 94

Quaker Folio

p. 95

* Elias Hicks, Jr.	* Arthur H. Howell	* Edward Tatnall	Amos James	* Benjamin Poultney
June 5, 1840-New York	June 19, 1840-Philadelphia	Brandywine, Delaware January 6, 1843-Philadelphia	(age 76 on Oct. 6, 1840) January 2, 1841-Baltimore	June 5, 1840-New York

p. 96

Mr. William T. Leggett	Mrs. William T. Leggett	Caleb Clothier	William N. Lacy	John Langdon
New York August 4, 1840-Saratoga	New York August 4, 1840-Saratoga	February 15, 1843-Philadelphia	February 7, 1843-Philadelphia	(age 87 on Aug. 22, 1842) June 22, 1842-Boston

*Silhouette missing

* **M. C. Pratt**	* **Watson J. Welding**	**Mr. William Lloyd**	**Micajah C. Pratt**	**Thomas Lloyd, Jr.**
Lynn, Mass.	March 5, 1841-Philadelphia	Philadelphia	Lynn, Mass.	October 28, 1840-Philadelphia
November 15, 1841-Boston		November 11, 1841-Boston	November 15, 1841-Boston	

Elias E. King	**Joseph King, Jr.**	**Francis T. King**	**Miles White**
December 3, 1840-Baltimore	December 3, 1840-Baltimore	December 3, 1840-Baltimore	Baltimore
			July 19, 1843-Saratoga Springs

*Silhouette missing

Quaker Folio

p. 99

Miss Mary E. King
December 3, 1840-Baltimore

Joseph King, Jr.
December 3, 1840-Baltimore

Tacy E. King
(Mrs. Joseph King)
December 3, 1840-Baltimore

T. King
December 3, 1840-Baltimore

p. 100

Mr. William E. Bartlett
December 14, 1840-Baltimore

Edward H. Stabler
December 14, 1840-Baltimore

Evan Thomas
Baltimore
July 18, 1843-Saratoga Springs

J. Ridgway
January 9, 1843-Philadelphia

Mr. P. E. Thomas
Baltimore
(nat. November 15, 1776)
December 5, 1842-Philadelphia

Quaker Folio

William M. Medcalfe
December 15, 1840-Baltimore

Lloyd Norris
(son-in-law to Mr. Tyson)
November 20, 1840-Baltimore

Samuel E. Tyson, M.D.
November 12, 1840-Baltimore

William Tyson
November 14, 1840-Baltimore

p. 101

Mrs. John D. Early
December 15, 1840-Baltimore

Anne George
(sister of Mrs. John Early)
November 26, 1840-Baltimore

Mrs. McPherson
April 10, 1841-Washington

Mary Ann Ellicott
November 26, 1840-Baltimore

p. 102

Quaker Folio

p. 103

* B. Wyatt Wistar	Mrs. Annabella C. Wistar	* Widow Sarah E. Cresson	Miss Sarah Pugh
Philadelphia	October 26, 1842	October 28, 1842-Philadelphia	April 22, 1843-Philadelphia
August 6, 1842-Saratoga			

p. 104

Mrs. Sarah W. Longstreth	Miss Elizabeth Wm. Abbott	Mrs. Lydia W. Price
"Barclay Hall," Philadelphia	(daughter of Sarah W. Longstreth)	(obt. July 10, 1843)
August 20, 1842-Saratoga	April 28, 1843	(daughter of Sarah W. Longstreth)
		April 28, 1843

*Silhouette missing

Quaker Folio

Mr. James P. Parke	**Miss Hannah Parke**	**Mr. William Hodgson**	**Charles J. Wistar**	**Anthony Morris Johnson**
December 12, 1842-Philadelphia	December 20, 1842-Philadelphia	Germantown	Germantown	Germantown
		April 13, 1843-Philadelphia	January 23, 1843-Philadelphia	March 31, 1843-Philadelphia

p. 105

Mr. Jonathan Palmer, Jr.	**Mrs. Sarah H. Palmer**	**Henry Palmer**	**Miss Sarah Palmer**
September 12, 1842-Philadelphia	(daughter of Isaac T. Hopper, page 56)	October 3, 1842	November 4, 1843-Philadelphia
	September 12, 1842-Philadelphia		

p. 106

Quaker Folio

p. 107

| **Mr. Edward Palmer** | **Peter I. Wright** | **Miss Fanny Palmer** | * **Charles Palmer** |
| January 3, 1843-Philadelphia | November 4, 1843-Philadelphia | November 4, 1843-Philadelphia | November 4, 1843-Philadelphia |

p. 108

Thomas Fisher
May 29, 1843-Philadelphia

George Gaskill
June 7, 1843-Burlington, New Jersey

Charles H. Abbott
April 24, 1843-Philadelphia

Samuel William Black
teacher
April 4, 1843-Philadelphia

* **J. B. Lippincott**
bookseller
April 8, 1843-Philadelphia

*Silhouette missing

Henry Albert Yardley
8 years
January 16, 1843-Philadelphia

Sarah S. Yardley
(aunt of Henry Albert Yardley
wife of W. Yardley, Sr.)
January 16, 1843-Philadelphia

William L. Yardley
11 years
January 16, 1843-Philadelphia

Mrs. Sarah S. Johnson
(mother of Miss H. S. Johnson)
February 3, 1843-Philadelphia

Miss H. S. Johnson
January 16, 1843-Philadelphia

Miss Hannah Wright
near Hudson, N.Y.
February 3, 1843-Philadelphia

p. 109

Mrs. Rebecca S. Folwell
(born July 23, 1762)
January 23, 1843-Philadelphia

William Folwell
(son of Rebecca)
February 13, 1843-Philadelphia

Joseph D. Folwell
(son of Mr. William Folwell)
February 13, 1843-Philadelphia

* **Mr. William Folwell**
February 13, 1843-Philadelphia

p. 110

*Silhouette missing

Quaker Folio

p. 111

Lewis P. Harvey
Delaware County, Pennsylvania
October 15, 1842-Philadelphia

Ellwood Harvey
medical student
October 5, 1842-Philadelphia

Miss Josephine S. Youle
October 5, 1842-Philadelphia

Chalkley Harvey
Chester County, Pennsylvania
January 13, 1843-Philadelphia

p. 112

John H. Warder
334 Arch Street
(Obt. Oct. 20, 1843)
October 20, 1842-Philadelphia

William G. Warder
334 Arch Street
October 20, 1842-Philadelphia

Miss Eleonor H. Warder
334 Arch Street
October 20, 1842-Philadelphia

Henrietta Warder
334 Arch Street
October 20, 1842-Philadelphia

Quaker Folio

p. 113

Professor John Griscom
Burlington
October 28, 1842-Philadelphia

Miss Ann Warder
October 20, 1842-Philadelphia

Henrietta Hoskins
October 11, 1842-Philadelphia

p. 114

Miss Gertrude Kimber
(now Mrs. Charles Burleigh)
abolitionist
"Kimberton," Chester County
October 12, 1842-Philadelphia

Miss Abigail Kimber
October 12, 1842-Philadelphia

Miss Sally F. Smith
October 7, 1842-Philadelphia

Widow Hannah Warder
(born Feb. 11, 1756)
January 19, 1843-Philadelphia

Quaker Folio

p. 115

* William H. Bacon	* Josiah Bacon	John Yarrow	John Bacon	George Martin
December 30, 1842-Philadelphia	December 30, 1842-Philadelphia	December 30, 1842-Philadelphia	January 13, 1843-Philadelphia	November 24, 1842-Philadelphia

p. 116

Mr. James Mott	Mrs. James Mott	Harry D. Landis	Elias Hicks
October 21, 1842-Philadelphia	October 21, 1842-Philadelphia	November 4, 1843-Philadelphia	(copied from woodcut at Philadelphia) October 7, 1843-Philadelphia

*Silhouette missing

Quaker Folio

* Alexander Cooper	* Miss Abby M. Cooper	John J. Walker	Samuel M. Day
October 19, 1842-New Jersey	October 1, 1842-Philadelphia	(brother page 79)	December 23, 1842-Philadelphia
		December 5, 1842-Philadelphia	

p. 117

* Sarah M. Coates	* John R. Coates counsellor-at-law	* Samuel Coates	* Morton Coates
(widow of John R. Coates)	(died 1842) age 61	manager of Pennsylvania Hospital	(son of John R. Coates)
December 17, 1842-Philadelphia	Agent to the estate of William Penn	(drawn by Leslie)-died June, 1830	April 14, 1843-Philadelphia
	cut from description and busts	(son of John R. Coates)	
	December 17, 1842-Philadelphia	December 17, 1842-Philadelphia	

* p. 118

Amy Coates (late wife of Samuel)
(mother of Joseph Saunders Coates)
cut as if age 40-obt. 1838, aged 71
taken by description

Joseph Saunders Coates
(Obt. 1836, about 56 years old)

p. 118½

*Silhouette missing

Quaker Folio

p. 119

                        Mr. Israel Cope   **William M. Collins**   **Mrs. Lydia C. Cope**
                      (born Nov. 11, 1770) (Lydia C. Cope's brother-in-law) January 14, 1843-Philadelphia
                  January 21, 1843-Philadelphia January 16, 1843-Philadelphia

*p. 120   * **Nathaniel Randolph**   * **George Randolph**   * **Edward Randolph, Jr.** taken by description   * **Richard Randolph**
           (son of Edward Randolph) (son of Edward Randolph) (50 years, died Dec. 1834) February 14, 1843-Philadelphia
           December 23, 1842-Philadelphia February 20, 1843-Philadelphia (father of Mrs. Richard D. Wood, page 123)
                                                           February 20, 1843-Philadelphia

p. 121

   Miss Jane F. Randolph   * **Miss Hannah F. Randolph**   * **George F. Randolph**   * **George F. Randolph**
   February 1, 1843-Philadelphia   January 17, 1843-Philadelphia   January 16, 1843-Philadelphia   January 16, 1843-Philadelphia

*Silhouette missing

Quaker Folio

p. 122

Mrs. Charles S. Wood	**Miss Elizabeth Wood**	**Charles S. Wood**	**G. Randolph Wood**	**Miss Hannah Wood**
(daughter of George F. Randolph, page 121)	January 19, 1843-Philadelphia	January 19, 1843-Philadelphia	January 19, 1843-Philadelphia	January 19, 1843-Philadelphia
January 19, 1843-Philadelphia				

p. 123

Mrs. Richard D. Wood
(daughter of Edward Randolph, page 120)
January 20, 1843-Philadelphia

Edward Randolph Wood
January 20, 1843-Philadelphia

| **Master Richard D. Wood** | **Infant** (under Mrs. Wood not named) | **Richard D. Wood** | **Mary Wood** | **Caroline Wood** |
| January 20, 1843-Philadelphia | January 20, 1843-Philadelphia | January 20, 1843-Philadelphia | January 20, 1843-Philadelphia | January 20, 1843-Philadelphia |

Quaker Folio

p. 124

Mrs. Hannah D. Wood
January 20, 1843-Philadelphia

Dr. George B. Wood
professor, University of Pennsylvania
January 20, 1843-Philadelphia

Mrs. C. H. Wood
January 20, 1843-Philadelphia

p. 125

Mr. Watson Jenks
January 28, 1843-Philadelphia

* Margaret T. Jenks
January 28, 1843-Philadelphia

Mrs. Julianna Jenks
January 28, 1843-Philadelphia

*Silhouette missing

Quaker Folio

p. 126

Mrs. Henry B. Tatham	Mr. Henry B. Tatham	Benjamin Tatham, Jr.	Miss Mary E. Morris	George N. Tatham
January 31, 1843-Philadelphia	January 31, 1843-Philadelphia	(cousin of Mary E. Morris) January 31, 1843-Philadelphia	Reading, Pennsylvania January 31, 1843-Philadelphia	January 31, 1843-Philadelphia

p. 127

Thomas N. Taylor	Miss Emma Louisa Taylor	Mr. F. Taylor	Miss Sarah Taylor	Dr. Thomas Allen, M.D.
Bristol, Bucks County, Pa. February 17, 1843-Philadelphia	February 13, 1843-Philadelphia	Bristol February 13, 1843-Philadelphia	(married Dr. Thomas Allen, M.D., 1845 from Attleboro, Bucks County, Pennsylvania) February 10, 1843-Philadelphia	Attleboro, Bucks County, Pennsylvania February 10, 1843-Philadelphia

Quaker Folio

p. 128

Miss Margaret Hart
February 2, 1843-Philadelphia

Miss Mary Hart
February 2, 1843-Philadelphia

Miss Rebecca S. Hart
February 3, 1843-Philadelphia

Miss Mary Davies
February 3, 1843-Philadelphia

p. 129

Mr. Thomas S. Cavender
November 8, 1843-Philadelphia

Mrs. M. L. Dawson
May 1, 1843-Philadelphia

Mr. M. L. Dawson
Director of the Public Schools,
Manager of Friends Asylum of Insane and
of the Colony Institution
May 1, 1843-Philadelphia

Quaker Folio

Isaiah Hacker
(uncle of W. Alfred Hacker)
May 1, 1843-Philadelphia

W. Alfred Hacker
May 12, 1843-Philadelphia

Isaac Hacker
February 8, 1843-Philadelphia

Henry M. Hacker
January 21, 1843-Philadelphia

Miss Esther S. Hacker
(sister of Henry Hacker)
(now wife of William Sharpless)
October 6, 1842-Philadelphia

p. 130

Albanus Smith (obt. 1842)
August 18, 1841-Saratoga

Lloyd P. Smith
January 9, 1844-New Orleans

* **Horace John Smith**

Robert P. Smith
9th Street above Locust, White House
7 Franklin Road
April 24, 1843-Philadelphia

p. 130½

*Silhouette missing

Quaker Folio

p. 131

Mrs. Mary Longstreth
(family on page 131½)
April 7, 1843-Philadelphia

Miss Anna S. Collins
(sister to Mary Longstreth and E. Pearsall)
April 7, 1843-Philadelphia

* **Mr. Robert Pearsall**
taken from description
(obt. Sept. 12, 1828, age 54)
March 24, 1843-Philadelphia

Mrs. Robert Pearsall
(late Miss Elizabeth Collins)
March 24, 1843-Philadelphia

p. 131½

Miss Susan Longstreth
January 30, 1843-Philadelphia

Elizabeth Morris
(wife of Israel Morris)
January 30, 1843-Philadelphia

Theodore (Israel) Morris
Philadelphia
July 20, 1844-Saratoga

Mr. William C. Longstreth
January 19, 1843-Philadelphia

Miss Mary Anna Longstreth
April 7, 1843-Philadelphia

* p. 132 * **Mrs. Emma C. Yarnall**
(daughter of Jasper Cope)
February 1, 1843-Philadelphia

* **Charles Yarnall**
February 1, 1843-Philadelphia

* **Ellis H. Yarnall**

* **Rebecca Cope, Jr.**
February 17, 1843

* **Mr. Jasper Cope**
(born April, 1775)
February 4, 1843-Philadelphia

* **Mrs. Jasper Cope**
February 4, 1843-Philadelphia

*Silhouette missing

Quaker Folio

Dr. Samuel George Morton, M.D.
October 31, 1843-Philadelphia

p. 132½

* **Miss Mary Stokes**
(niece of T. P. Cope)
March 16, 1843-Philadelphia

* **Thomas P. Cope**
March 16, 1843-Philadelphia

* p. 133

| **Miss Mary C. Jones** | **Mr. Isaac C. Jones** | **William F. Jones** | **Mrs. H. Jones** |
| March 4, 1843-Philadelphia | March 4, 1843-Philadelphia | March 4, 1843-Philadelphia | March 4, 1843-Philadelphia |

p. 134

*Silhouette missing

Quaker Folio

p. 135

Miss Martha Hooton
February 6, 1843-Philadelphia

Miss Elizabeth Hooton
March 17, 1843-Philadelphia

Miss Hannah E. Jones
March 4, 1843-Philadelphia

Franklin C. Jones
March 4, 1843-Philadelphia

p. 136

Mr. Joshua Barker
(obt. Feb. 6, 1843-67 years)
(brother of Mrs. Martha Hilles)
(taken after death)
February 7, 1843-Philadelphia

Mrs. Martha Hilles
(wife of Eli Hilles of Wilmington)
February 7, 1843-Philadelphia

* p. 136½

* **Joshua Clibborn Nicholson**
September 20, 1843-New York

* **Mrs. M. Nicholson**
September 20, 1843-New York

* **Meadows T. Nicholson**
September 20, 1843-New York

*Silhouette missing

Quaker Folio

* Josiah Clibborn	* Adele B. Clibborn	* Mr. Joshua Clibborn	* Mr. Joshua Clibborn
September 8, 1843-New York	September 8, 1843-New York	September 8, 1843-New York	September 8, 1843-New York

* p. 137

p. 138

Mrs. S. N. Dickinson
(sister to Mrs. A. C. Logan, "Stenton")
March 9, 1843-Philadelphia

Mr. A. C. Logan
"Stenton"
March 22, 1843-Philadelphia

Mrs. A. C. Logan (Maria D.)
"Stenton"
March 22, 1843-Philadelphia

p. 139

William Hunt
April 21, 1843-Philadelphia

Mr. Thomas Firth
(brother of Mrs. Isaac C. Jones, page 134)
March 14, 1843-Philadelphia

Dr. J. D. Logan, M.D.
"Stenton"
March 15, 1843-Philadelphia

Gustavus Logan
"Stenton"
March 15, 1843-Philadelphia

Miss Mary N. Logan
March 15, 1843-Philadelphia

*Silhouette missing

Quaker Folio

p. 140

Mr. Thomas Gilpin
February 20, 1843-Philadelphia

Mr. John Bonsall
April 3, 1843-Philadelphia

Joseph Maxfield
May 3, 1843-Philadelphia

p. 141

Mr. George Truman
105 Arch Street
March 20, 1843-Philadelphia

Mrs. George Truman (Catherine H.)
105 Arch Street
March 20, 1843-Philadelphia

Mr. Thomas S. Newlin
April 3, 1843-Philadelphia

* **Mrs. Thomas S. Newlin (Catherine)**
April 3, 1843-Philadelphia

*Silhouette missing

Quaker Folio

p. 142

Sarah Jackson
(born Feb. 28, 1784)
(widow of Richard Jackson)
April 11, 1843-Philadelphia

Hannah Zell
(born Feb. 19, 1790)
(wife of Thomas Zell)
April 29, 1843-Philadelphia

Mrs. John Farnum
April 7, 1843-Philadelphia

Mr. John Farnum
April 7, 1843-Philadelphia

p. 143

Paschall Morris
Chester County
March 25, 1843-Philadelphia

Mrs. Lydia P. Thompson
(wife of James B. Thompson)
March 30, 1843-Philadelphia

*Silhouette missing

Quaker Folio

p. 144

E. K. K. Wetherill
August 5, 1843-Saratoga

Rachel Wetherill
Saratoga
August 5, 1843-Philadelphia

John Price Wetherill
August 20, 1842-Saratoga

p. 144 1/2

John M. Wetherill
(nephew of John Price Wetherill, page 144)
August 20, 1842-Saratoga

Joseph B. Wetherill
(nephew of John Price Wetherill, page 144)
August 20, 1842-Saratoga

*Silhouette missing

Dr. William Wetherill April 12, 1843-Philadelphia	**Mrs. William Wetherill** (daughter of Isabella Bloomfield) April 12, 1843-Philadelphia	**Mrs. Isabella Bloomfield,** relict (relative of Major General Joseph Bloomfield) April 13, 1843-Philadelphia	**Miss Rachel Wetherill** April 13, 1843-Philadelphia	**Samuel Wetherill** April 13, 1843-Philadelphia	p. 145
* **Emilie Vaux** April 20, 1843-Philadelphia	* **Eliza H. Vaux,** widow April 20, 1843-Philadelphia	* **Annie Vaux,** (no. 2) April 20, 1843-Philadelphia	* **Elizabeth Vaux** April 20, 1843-Philadelphia	* **William S. Vaux** April 20, 1843-Philadelphia	* p. 146

George Vaux April 20, 1843-Philadelphia	**Miss Frances Vaux,** (no. 3) April 20, 1843-Philadelphia	* **Miss Hannah S. Vaux** April 20, 1843-Philadelphia	* **Miss Mary Emlen Vaux** (obt. Aug. 29, 1844) April 20, 1843-Philadelphia	**Mrs. Susan V. Cresson** (late Miss Vaux) April 20, 1843-Philadelphia	p. 146½

*Silhouette missing

Quaker Folio

*p. 147
    * **Miss Hannah Sansom**
May 3, 1843-Philadelphia

    * **Mrs. Susan Sansom** widow
(born Dec. 5, 1776)
(mother of Mrs. Eliza H. Vaux, page 146)
May 3, 1843-Philadelphia

p. 148

Miss Sarah English
314 Walnut Street
August 14, 1843-Philadelphia

Samuel English
314 Walnut Street
August 14, 1843-Philadelphia

p. 149

Mrs. Sarah Pennock
(74 years in 1843)
May 22, 1843-Philadelphia

Sarah Pennock
May 22, 1843-Philadelphia

Miss Isabella L. Pennock
May 22, 1843-Philadelphia

Dog On Chair

Caroline Pennock
(wife of C. Wistar Pennock, M.D.)
[c.p. char. book folio, page 86½]
May 22, 1843-Philadelphia

*Silhouette missing

Quaker Folio

Miss Hannah Embree	**Miss Hannah P. Davis**	**Rebecca Embree**	* **Sibbilla Embree**
April 29, 1843-Philadelphia	West Chester April 28, 1843-Philadelphia	March 11, 1843-Philadelphia	April 26, 1843-Philadelphia

p. 150

Mr. Philip M. Price **Mrs. Philip M. Price**
October 14, 1845-Philadelphia October 14, 1845-Philadelphia

p. 150½

*Silhouette missing

Quaker Folio

p. 151

Mr. Eli K. Price	**Sibbylla E. Price**	**Mary Ferris Price** 7 years	**Mrs. Eli K. Price**	**Mrs. Mary Embree**
counsellor at law	(born March 31, 1834)	(daughter of Philip M. Price, page 150½)	(late Miss Anne Embree)	(widow of Jesse Embree)
May 10, 1843-Philadelphia	May 10, 1843-Philadelphia	May 10, 1843-Philadelphia	May 10, 1843-Philadelphia	May 10, 1843-Philadelphia

p. 152

* **Charles W. Wharton**	**Rodman Wharton**	**William Wharton**	* **William Wharton, Jr.**	* **Deborah F. Wharton**
September 22, 1842-Philadelphia	September 22, 1842-Philadelphia	Philadelphia	1843-Saratoga Springs	July 25, 1843-Saratoga Springs
		July 25, 1843-Saratoga Springs		

*Silhouette missing

Quaker Folio

p. 152½

Silvanus J. Macy	* William H. Macy, Jr.	* George Trimble Macy
February 18, 1845-New York	February 18, 1845-New York	February 18, 1845-New York

p. 153

* Mary J. Macy	Josiah Macy, Jr.	Cornelia T. Macy	Mrs. Eliza L. Macy	William H. Macy
New York—(5′ 2″ tall)	New York	New York—(4′ 8″ tall)	New York	(5′ 10″ tall)
August 13, 1844-Saratoga	August 13, 1844-Saratoga	August 13, 1844-Saratoga	August 13, 1844-Saratoga	August 13, 1844-Saratoga

*Silhouette missing

Quaker Folio

p. 154

Unnamed
(sister of Mrs. E. P. Newbold)
September 10, 1844-Saratoga

Miss Charlotte Newbold
Greenfield, New Jersey
September 10, 1844-Saratoga

William F. Newbold
Greenfield, New Jersey
September 10, 1844-Saratoga

Mrs. E. P. Newbold
September 9, 1844-Saratoga

p. 155

James Cresson
(born Oct. 1, 1776—obt. June, 1843)
May 12, 1843-Philadelphia

Mrs. Sarah Cresson
(born, July, 1771)
May 12, 1843-Philadelphia

Mrs. Martha W. Walker
(daughter of James Cresson)
(daughter-in-law of Lewis Walker)
May 12, 1843-Philadelphia

Lewis Walker
(born Nov. 19, 1767)
May 12, 1843-Philadelphia

Quaker Folio

p. 156

* Walter Cresson	* John H. Cresson	Benjamin M. Hollinshead
(son of John H.)	May 12, 1843-Philadelphia	October 9, 1843-Philadelphia
May 8, 1843-Philadelphia		

p. 157

Miss Jane Chapman	Mr. Joseph Cresson, Jr.
(sister of Mrs. Joseph Cresson)	May 16, 1843-Philadelphia
May 16, 1843-Philadelphia	

*Silhouette missing

Quaker Folio

p. 157½

Mr. Joseph Cresson	**Mrs. Mercy Cresson**	**Miss Rebecca G. Cresson**	**Miss Mercy Anna Cresson**
May 12, 1843-Philadelphia	(born May 13, 1791)	May 12, 1843-Philadelphia	May 12, 1843-Philadelphia
	May 12, 1843-Philadelphia		

p. 158

Mercy Anna Fraley, 3 years
May 13, 1843-Philadelphia

Elizabeth Fraley
May 13, 1843-Philadelphia

Mrs. Jane C. Fraley (born 1810)
(wife of Frederick Fraley—American Character Book page 47½)
(daughter of J. Cresson, page 157)
May 13, 1843-Philadelphia

Sarah C. Fraley
9 years 10 months
May 13, 1843-Philadelphia

Mr. C. M. Cresson
(son of John C., page 159)
May 13, 1843-Philadelphia

Charles Massey, Jr. (born April 14, 1778)
Port member of council, Warden of Philadelphia
(father of Letitia L. Cresson)
May 15, 1843-Philadelphia

Mrs. Letitia L. Cresson
(wife of John C. Cresson)
May 15, 1843-Philadelphia

Mr. John C. Cresson
May 15, 1843-Philadelphia

p. 159

Mrs. R. Wistar
July 13, 1843-Saratoga

Miss Sarah Wistar
July 13, 1843-Saratoga

Mr. R. Wistar
July 13, 1843-Saratoga

p. 160

Quaker Folio

p. 160½

Mrs. R. L. Wistar
July 13, 1843-Saratoga

Richard Wistar
August 23, 1844-Saratoga

p. 161
Blank

p. 162

George Delwyn (Dillwyn)
(copied from engraving)
May 10, 1843-Philadelphia

John Cox (born Feb. 23, 1754)
(Oxinead on cord near Burlington, N.J.)
June 3, 1843-Philadelphia

John Cox
(pasted label with signature "John Cox, Feb. 23")
June 3, 1843-Philadelphia

Dr. Joseph Parrish
surgeon of Pennsylvania Hospital
taken from busts and description
(obt. March 18, 1840 at 61 years)
(attended John Randolph of Roanoke)
(father of 11 children)
May 10, 1843-Philadelphia

Quaker Folio

p. 163

Mrs. Elizabeth Robeson (age 76)
June 15, 1843-Philadelphia

Sarah Robeson
(born April 25, 1771)
June 15, 1843-Philadelphia

Mary Bonsall
June 16, 1843-Philadelphia

p. 164

Mrs. Joseph Lea
(sister of Jonathan Robeson)
October 15, 1843-Philadelphia

Mr. Jonathan Robeson
October 15, 1843-Philadelphia

Catherine Moore
(born Nov. 28, 1791)
(sister of Jonathan Robeson)
June 15, 1843-Philadelphia

Mr. Joseph Lea
October 15, 1843-Philadelphia

Quaker Folio

p. 164½

John R. Moore	* Catherine M. Mather	Mrs. Ann W. Mather
"Robeson Mill"	(born April 4, 1841)	(daughter of Mrs. Catherine Moore, page 164)
(son of Mrs. Catherine Moore)	June 17, 1843-Philadelphia	June 17, 1843-Philadelphia
June 16, 1843-Philadelphia		

p. 165

Miss Catherine Lea, (no. 2)	Miss Elizabeth Lea, (no. 2)	Joseph Lea, Jr.	Joseph Lea, Sr.
(5′ 5½″ tall)	(5′ 2″ tall)	October 14, 1843-Philadelphia	"Milverton," near Philadelphia
June 13, 1843-Philadelphia	June 13, 1843-Philadelphia		October 14, 1843-Philadelphia

*Silhouette missing

Quaker Folio

Mrs. Joseph Lea, Sr.	**Miss Anna R. Lea**	**Miss Sarah Lea,** (no. 2)	**Miss Frances Lea**
"Milverton"	"Milverton"	"Milverton"	"Milverton"
June 16, 1843-Philadelphia	June 16, 1843-Philadelphia	June 16, 1843-Philadelphia	(now Mrs. Edmund Burke Smith)
			June 16, 1843-Philadelphia

p. 166

Miss Jane P. Lea	**Miss Martha R. Lea**	**Miss Ellenor R. Lea**	**Mr. Edmund Burke Smith**	**Mrs. Edmund Burke Smith**
"Milverton"	"Milverton"	"Milverton"	"Milverton"	"Milverton"
June 16, 1843-Philadelphia	June 16, 1843-Philadelphia	June 16, 1843-Philadelphia	June 16, 1843-Philadelphia	(late Frances Lea, page 166)
				June 16, 1843-Philadelphia

p. 167

Quaker Folio

p. 168

Mr. Thomas T. Lea	**Miss Sally A. Lea**	**Miss Mary C. Lea**	* **Mrs. Frances C. Lea**
June 16, 1843-Philadelphia	June 16, 1843-Philadelphia	June 16, 1843-Philadelphia	June 16, 1843-Philadelphia

* p. 168½   * **Mary Lavarell**
(nurse in Mrs. T. Lea's family)

p. 169

William R. Robeson	**Mr. George Minster**	**Emily Minster**	**Joseph Lea Minster**	**Mrs. George Minster**
Fall River, Mass.	June 15, 1843-"Milverton"	(baby at top of page)	(baby on pillow)	June 15, 1843-"Milverton"
October 21, 1843-Philadelphia		June 15, 1843-"Milverton"	June 15, 1843-"Milverton"	

*Silhouette missing

Joseph Tatnall Lea	Robeson Lea	Miss Ellen H. Lea	Richard M. Lea	Thomas T. Lea, Jr.	Mrs. Robeson Lea
June 17, 1843-Philadelphia	June 17, 1843-Philadelphia	(obt. 1843) June 17, 1843-Philadelphia	June 17, 1843-Philadelphia	(born April 19, 1843) June 17, 1843-Philadelphia	June 17, 1843-Philadelphia

p. 170

Miss Susan Massey	R. V. Massey	Benjamin Ferris	Thomas Eddy
(Now Mrs. Joseph Lea) October 25, 1843-Philadelphia	Philadelphia July 6, 1844-Saratoga	Wilmington, Delaware March 1, 1845-New York	February 25, 1845-New York

p. 171

Quaker Folio

p. 172

Mr. Jabez M. Fisher	**Mrs. Jabez M. Fisher**	**Mrs. Sarah R. Fisher**	**Miss Annie W. Fisher**
engineer	November 2, 1843-Philadelphia	(87 years)	New York
November 2, 1843-Philadelphia		November 2, 1843-Philadelphia	November 2, 1843-Philadelphia

p. 173

Miers F. Warner	**Redwood Warner**	**Miss Sally Warner**	**Mrs. Lydia Warner**	**Mr. Joseph Warner**
November 2, 1843-Philadelphia	August 12, 1840-Philadelphia	August 12, 1840-Philadelphia	(wife of Joseph Warner)	January 11, 1843-Philadelphia
			November 2, 1843-Philadelphia	

Quaker Folio

p. 174
Blank

p. 175

Unnamed Bust of Lady

Catherine H. Inman
March 21, 1843-Philadelphia

Jane Jackson Darby
May 29, 1840-New York

pp. 176–203
Blank

This concludes the Quaker silhouettes taken from life by Edouart in England and America between 1827–1845. The following pages, 204–206, are profiles of some of the most respected early leaders of the Society of Friends. Edouart kept these patterns taken from lithographs, busts, portraits, or cuttings by other artists for patrons to preserve in family albums.

Quaker Folio

Historical Quaker Leaders

p. 204

Thomas Scattergood
Philanthropist
(Earliest introducer of the
System of Mutual Instruction)

* **Dr. John Wakely Lettson**
Emminent Philosopher
(London—obt. 1825)

William Rawle
Counsellor—(obt. Oct. 1833)
(U.S. Prosecuting Attorney, appointed by Washington)

p. 204½

* **Samuel Shoemaker**
Mayor of Philadelphia (age 70)

Richard Smith
Burlington—(age 50)

William Willson

Thomas Harrison
Advocate General Emancipation

Daniel Williams, Esquire
(age 70)

James Maylor
(from original by late Dr. Preston)

Robert Proud
Author of the History of Pennsylvania

John Head

* **Samuel Coats**
Governor of Hospital

* **Joshua Howell**
(obt. 1800)

Owen Jones
(age 78)

Dr. J. D. Griffiths
(obt. 1828—65 years)

*Silhouette missing

Quaker Folio

p. 205

Sarah Rhoads (Roads)	* Mary Ridgway	George Delwyn (Dillwyn)	Rebecca Jones	* John Pemberton
	Minister in the Society—(age 67)	Minister in the Society (age 80)	Minister in the Society—(age 50)	Minister in the Society—(age 63)
* Nicholas Waln	John Joseph Gurney	William Savery	Thomas Shillitoe	* James Pemberton
Counsellor at Law	Minister in the Society	Minister in the Society—(age 40)	Minister in the Society	(age 63)
Minister in the Society			(age 82)—(died June 12, 1836)—from England	

* **Daniel Wheeler**
Minister and Missionary to Russia
(obt. May, 1841—67 years)

p. 206

* Mary Pleasant	* Samuel Pleasant	* Isaac Zane	* John Field	George Warner	Josiah Hewes
wife of Samuel	Emt. Marshall—(obt. 1810)	Rev. on Time(?)	(obt. March 1815)	(died at 98 years)	Brother to the Signer of the Declaration of Independence

* **Richard Smith**   **John Drinker**   * **Thomas Paschall**
Delegate to the first Congress   Cashier of North American Bank   merchant in 1780
(during the Revolution)

*Silhouette missing

Newspaper Articles

Edouart often clipped notices about his sitters years after the cutting.

p. 8

Nathaniel Hartland, Esquire

Newspaper clipping—February 6, 1837:
"In the 87th year of her age Rebecca relict of Nathaniel Hartland, Esq., of Tewkesbury, a highly respectable member of the Society of Friends and a lady of the kindest and most benevolent disposition."

p. 9

John Allis Hartland, Esquire

Newspaper clipping—July, 1838:
"In our paper of last week we recorded the death of John Allis Hartland, Esquire of Tewkesbury. We are now requested by a correspondent to add that the interment of this highly respected gentleman took place on Tuesday the 3rd inst. in the burial grounds attached to the meeting house of the Society of Friends in the town. Upward of fifty members of the Society of Friends and nearly two hundred gentlemen and tradesmen of the town and neighborhood followed the body in procession to the grave and the greater part of the shops were kept closed during the day as token of respect to the memory of the deceased."

p. 28

Tobias Pim

Newspaper article, Sept. 25, 1838:
"On the 25th ult., at the residence of his father, Pakenham-place, after a tedious illness, Tobias Pim, age 24 years. His amiable deportment, and engaging desposition won for him the love and esteem of his many relatives and aquaintances.

   Triumphant in thy closing eye,
     The hope of glory shown;
   Joy breaths in thy expiring sigh,
     To think the fight was won.
   Gently the passing spirit fled,
     Sustained by grace divine.—
   Oh! may such grace on us be shed,
     And make our end like thine!"

p. 32

Miss Charlotte Webb

Newspaper article, October, 1838:
"On the 30th ult. scarletina in her fifth year, Charlotte, youngest daughter of William Webb of Belfast."

p. 49

*Samuel Metford

Newspaper article, July 4, 1844:
"Drowned while bathing, Samuel and Thomas Metford, age respectively 26 and 28 years and members of the Society of Friends were bathing yesterday off Fort Hamilton, L.I., and unfortunately went out over their depth and before assistance could be rendered them, were drowned. We understand that they were natives of Bristol, England. Their bodies were recovered, and will be interred this afternoon."

p. 65

Stacy B. Collins

Newspaper Article:
At Friends' meeting, Arch Street on 2d inst., Stacy B. Collins, of New York, to Hannah W., daughter of Joseph R. Jenks of Philadelphia.

p. 129

M. L. Dawson

Newspaper article, May 1, 1843:
The mayor reappointed Isaac Elliott and M. L. Dawson managers of the House of Refuge.

*Silhouette missing

Joseph Lea, Sr.

(*actual size*)

Mr. Lea of "Milverton" pauses from reading his newspaper to converse with the family. His duplicate is on page 165 in the folio and in framed and finished on page 115.

Charlotte Temple Knowles
(actual size)

Charlotte was born a slave and later became the servant of Mrs. Cooledge. Edouart cut her shadow in October, 1839. Her duplicates are on page 50 and 50½.

Alphabetical Listing of Edouart's Quaker Folio
Friends Historical Library, of Swarthmore College

Abbott, Charles H., 108
Abbott, Miss Elizabeth William, 104
Abel, Abraham, 14
*Alexander, Mrs. Samuel, 33
Allen, Dr. Thomas, 127
Allen, William Bell, 19
Allis, Jacob (2 poses), 7
Andrews, John H., 66

Bacon, John, 115
*Bacon, Josiah, 115
*Bacon, William H., 115
Baker, Mrs. Dobel, 58
Baker, George Corlies, 59
Baker, Sarah H., 58½
*Bakewell, Miss Mary, 26
Ball, Dr. Joseph (2 poses), 4
Ball, Richard, Esquire (3 poses), 4
*Barcroft, Mr. Joseph, 33
*Barcroft, Mrs. Joseph, 33
Barker, Mr. Joshua, 136
*Barker, Priscilla, 43
Barney, Mrs. Peter (Eliza), 87
Barrow, Henry H., 83
Barrow, Master Henry, 83
Bartlett, Mr. William E., 100
*Bell, Abraham, 52
Bell, Miss Anne Eliza, 52½B
Bell, James C., 52
Bell, Miss Mary, 53
*Bell, Miss Mary, 33
*Bell, Mrs. Mary, 35
*Bell, Miss Rebecca (Mrs. Harvey), 53
Bell, Mr. Thomas C., 53
Bell, Mrs. Thomas C., 53
Bell, William, 52, 52½ A
Binns, William, 75
Binns, Mrs. William, 75
Black, Samuel William, 108
Bloomfield, Mrs. Isabella, 145
Bonsall, Mr. John, 140
Bonsall, Mary, 163
*Bowne, Hugh H., 84
Brainard, Julius, 44½
*Brainard, Mrs. Julius, 45
*Breed, Lucy J., 86
Breed, Sarah S., 86
*Breed, Mrs. Sarah S., 86
*Brown, Charles, 44
*Brown, Ed O., 44
Brown, Isaac H., 56½ A
*Brown, Jeremiah, 44
*Brown, Mrs. Jeremiah, 44
*Brown, John M., 44
Buffum, Mr. James N., 87
Burlingham, Richard, 22½B

Carpenter, William S., 82
Cavender, Mr. Thomas S., 129
Chapman, Miss Jane, 157
Cheesman, Miss Ann, 80
*Cheesman, Dr. J. C., 80
*Cheesman, Mrs. J. C., 80
Cheesman, J. C., Junior, 80

*Churchman, Pennell, 84
Clapp, Otis, 93
Clapp, Samuel H., 83
*Clapp, Sillas, 82
Clarke, Miss Ellen, 23
Clarke, Mr. Joseph, 23
Clarke, Mrs. Joseph, 23
Clarke, Lucy, 19
Clarke, Miss Sarah, 23
*Clibborn, Adele, 137
*Clibborn, Josiah, 137
*Clibborn, Mr. Joshua, 137
*Clibborn, Mr. Joshua, 137
Clothier, Caleb, 96
Coates, Amy, 118½
*Coates, John R., 118
Coates, Joseph Saunders, 118½
*Coates, Morton, 118
*Coates, Samuel, 118, 204½
*Coates, Sarah M., 118
COCK—see also Cox
Cock, Elizabeth R., 91
Cock, Dr. Thomas, 90½, *91
Cock, Mrs. Thomas, 90½, *91
Collins, Abel Francis, 92
Collins, Miss Anna S., 131
Collins, B. S., 64½
Collins, Charles, 64½
Collins, Miss Hannah N., 66
Collins, Isaac, 65
Collins, Mr. Joseph B., 64½
Collins, Rebecca, 66
Collins, Mr. Stacy B., 65
Collins, Mrs. Stacy B. (Hannah), 65
Collins, Thomas, 65
Collins, William M., 119
*Comstock, Phebe Anna, 90
*Congdon, Gilbert, 81
Congdon, Mr. Welcome, 81
*Conran, Mr. John, 27
Cooke, William, 19
*Cooledge, Daniel, 48
*Cooledge, Mrs. Daniel, 49
Cooledge, Mr. George, 50
*Cooledge, William J., Jr., 49
*Cooper, Miss Abby M., 117
*Cooper, Alexander, 117
Cope, Mr. Israel, 119
*Cope, Mr. Jasper, 132
*Cope, Mrs. Jasper, 132
Cope, Mrs. Lydia C., 119
*Cope, Rebecca, Jr., 132
*Cope, Thomas P., 133
Corlies, Mrs. Margaret G., 59
Corlies, Mrs. Patience, 58
*Cornell, Elijah, 74
Cornell, Mrs. Elijah, 74
Cornell, Miss, 74
Cowdrey, Samuel F., 93
COX—see also Cock
Cox, Benjamin, 72
*Cox, Charles, 73
Cox, John (2 poses), 162
Cox, Susan, 72

*Cox, William Henry, 72
Cresson, Mr. C. M., 158
Cresson, James, 155
Cresson, Mr. John C., 159
*Cresson, John H., 156
Cresson, Mr. Joseph, 157½
Cresson, Mr. Joseph, Jr., 157
Cresson, Mrs. Letitia L., 159
Cresson, Mrs. Mercy, 157½
Cresson, Miss Mercy Anna, 157½
Cresson, Miss Rebecca G., 157½
Cresson, Mrs. Sarah, 155
*Cresson, Widow Sarah E., 103
Cresson, Mrs. Susan V., 146½
*Cresson, Walter, 156

Darby, Jane Jackson, 175
Davies, Miss Mary, 128
Davis, Hannah P., 150
Dawson, Miss Charlotte, 34
Dawson, Mr. M. L., 129
Dawson, Mrs. M. L., 129
*Day, Mablon, 68
Day, Samuel M., 117
Delwyn, George, 162, 205
See also Dillwyn
Dibble, Mrs. Daniel D. T. (Ann), 85
*Dibble, Master Edward, 85
Dickinson, Mrs. S. N., 138
*Dickinson, Samuel, 25
Dillwyn, George, 162, 205
Dog on chair, 149
Drinker, John, 206

Earle, Phebe, 88
Early, Mrs. John D., 102
Eddy, Thomas, 171
Ellicott, Mary Ann, 102
Embree, Hannah, 150
Embree, Mrs. Mary, 151
Embree, Rebecca, 150
*Embree, Sibbilla, 150
English, Samuel, 148
English, Miss Sarah, 148

Farnum, Mr. John, 142
Farnum, Mrs. John, 142
*Farrer, Miss Anne, 3
Ferris, Benjamin, 171
*Field, John, 206
Firth, Mr. Thomas, 139
Fisher, Miss Annie W., 172
Fisher, Mr. Jabez M., 172
Fisher, Mrs. Jabez M., 172
Fisher, Mrs. Sarah R., 172
Fisher, Thomas, 108
Folwell, Joseph D., 110
Folwell, Mrs. Rebecca S., 110
Folwell, William, 110
*Folwell, Mr. William, 110
Fraley, Elizabeth, 158
Fraley, Mrs. Jane C., 158
Fraley, Mercy Anna, 158
Fraley, Sarah C., 158

*Silhouette missing

The names of the sitters and the pages correspond to the numbers Edouart used in the Quaker Duplicate Book.

*Freeth, Miss Lucy, 26
*Freeth, Mrs. Lucy, 26

*Gaines, Mrs. Stephen, 71
Gaskill, George, 108
George, Anne, 102
*Gibbons, Mrs. Abigail H., 57
*Gibbons, James L., 57
*Gibbons, Julia, 56½B
*Gibbons, Lucy, 56½B
*Gibbons, Sarah, 57
*Gibbons, William, 57
Gill, Timothi, Esquire, 25
Gilpin, Mr. Thomas, 140
Goodere, Miss, 7
Goodere, Moses, 7
*Graves, Miss, 10
Greer, Miss Eliza, 31
Greer, Mrs. Samuel (Jane), 31
*Grellet, Miss Rachel, 1½
*Grellet, Stephen, 1½
Griffiths, Dr. J. D., 204½
*Griften, John, 71
Griften, Solomon, 64
Griscom, Professor John, 113
Gurney, John Joseph, 205

Hacker, Miss Esther S., 130
Hacker, Henry M., 130
Hacker, Isaac, 130
Hacker, Isaiah, 130
Hacker, W. Alfred, 130
*Haight, Samuel L., 84
*Halsted, C. L., 84
*Hargrave, Miss Caroline, 21
Hargrave, Henry, 21
Hargrave, Miss Louisa, 21
*Hargrave, Mr. William, 21
*Hargrave, Mrs. William, 21
Harris, Miss Ann E., 89
*Harris, Edwards, 1
Harrison, Thomas, 204½
Hart, Miss Margaret, 128
Hart, Miss Mary, 128
Hart, Miss Rebecca S., 128
Hartland, Alfred Harford, 8½
Hartland, Anna, 9
Hartland, John Allis, (3 poses), 9
Hartland, Nathaniel (2 poses), 8
Hartland, Rebecca, 8
Harvey, Chalkley, 111
Harvey, Ellwood 111
Harvey, Lewis P., 111
Harvey, Miss Marguerite (2 poses), 36
*Harvey, Mr. William, 36
Hawxhurst, Mrs. Hannah, 61
Hawxhurst, Mrs. Sarah C., 64½
Hawxhurst, Thomas (2 poses), 62
Haydock, Mr. George G., 42
Haydock, Hannah Wharton, 42
Haydock, Mary, 42
Haydock, Robert, Jr., 42
*Haydock, Samuel, Sr., 42
Head, John, 204½
Hewes, Josiah, 206
Hicks, Elias, 116
*Hicks, Elias, Jr., 95
Hilles, Mrs. Martha, 136
Hinsdale, Stephens G., 83
Hodgson, Mr. William, 105
Holdship, Mrs., 2
Hollinshead, Benjamin M., 156
Hooton, Miss Elizabeth, 135
Hooton, Miss Martha, 135

Hopkins, Thomas, 94
Hopper, Edward, 56
Hopper, Isaac T., 56, 56½ A
Hopper, John Jr., 56
Hopper, Dr. Josiah, 56½
Hoskins, Henrietta, 113
*Hotaling, Mr. Leonard G., 45
*Hotaling, Mrs. Leonard G., 45
Howe, Josiah, 93
*Howell, Arthur H., 95
*Howell, Joshua, 204½
*Howell, Rebecca, 26
*Howland, Charles V., 63
*Howland, Mr. Mathew, 63
*Howland, Mrs. Mathew, 63
Hull, Miss Henrietta, 85
Hull Rebecca, 85
Hull, Wager, 43
Hunt, William, 139

Inman, Catherine H., 175

*Jackson, Georgiana Eliza, 19
Jackson, Miss Jane, 53
Jackson, John Pim, 19
Jackson, Sarah, 142
James, Amos, 95
*Janney, Mr. Phinneas, 64
*Janney, Mrs. Phinneas (Sarah), 64
Jenks, Mrs. Julianna, 125
*Jenks, Margaret T., 125
Jenks, Mr. Watson, 125
Jenkins, Silvanus T., 54
Jenkins, William, 87
Johnson, Anthony Morris, 105
Johnson, Miss H. S., 109
Johnson, Miss Isabella, 94
Johnson, Miss Martha Ann, 94
Johnson, Sarah S., 109
Jones, Franklin C., 135
Jones, Mrs. H., 134
Jones, Miss Hannah E., 135
Jones, Mr. Isaac C., 134
Jones, Miss Mary C., 134
Jones, Owen, 204½
Jones, Rebecca, 205
Jones, William F., 134
Justice, Miss Caroline, 46½
Justice, Miss Elizabeth, 47
Justice, George, 47
Justice, Mr. George N., 47
Justice, Mrs. George N. (Esther), 47
Justice, Rudolph, 47

Kimber, Miss Abigail, 114
Kimber, Miss Gertrude, 114
King, Elias E., 98
King, Francis T., 98
King, Joseph, Jr., 98, 99
King, Miss Mary E., 99
King, Mr. T., 99
King, Mrs. Tacy E., 99
Knight, Henry, Esquire, 2
Knowles, Charlotte Temple, 50, 50½

Lacy, William N., 96
Lamb, Mrs. Thomas, 32
Landis, Harry D., 116
Langdon, John, 96
*Lavarell, Mary, 168½
Lavender, Mrs. Sarah R., 74
Lea, Miss Anna R., 166
Lea, Miss Catherine M., 46, 165
Lea, Miss Elizabeth, 165

Lea, Miss Ellen H., 170
Lea, Miss Ellenor R., 167
Lea, Miss Frances, 166
*Lea, Mrs. Frances C., 168
Lea, Miss Jane P., 167
Lea, Mr. Joseph, 164
Lea Joseph, Jr., 46, 165
Lea, Joseph, Sr., 46, 165
Lea, Mrs. Joseph, 164
Lea, Mrs. Joseph, Sr., 166
Lea, Joseph Tatnall, 170
Lea, Miss Martha R., 167
Lea, Miss Mary C., 168
Lea, Richard M., 170
Lea, Robeson, 170
Lea, Mrs. Robeson, 170
Lea, Miss Sally A., 168
Lea, Miss Sarah, 166
Lea, Mr. Thomas T., 168
Lea, Thomas T., Jr., 170
Leggett, Aaron, 89
Leggett, Anne T., 58
Leggett, Miss Martha, 89
Leggett, Mrs. Thomas (Patience), 58
Leggett, Thomas, Jr., 59
Leggett, Mr. Walter T., 59
Leggett, Mr. William T., 96
Leggett, Mrs. William T., 96
*Lettson, Dr. John Wakley, 204
Lewis John T., 93
Lewis, Mordecai, 93
*Lippincott, J. B., 108
Logan, Mr. A. C., 138
Logan, Gustavus, 139
Logan, Dr. J. D., 139
Logan, Mrs. Maria D., 138
Logan, Miss Mary N., 139
Lloyd, Thomas, Jr., 97
Lloyd, Mr. William, 97
Longstreth, Mrs. Mary, 131
Longstreth, Miss Mary Anna, 131½
Longstreth, Mrs. Sarah W., 104
Longstreth, Miss Susan, 131½
Longstreth, Mr. William C., 131½

McCarty, Camilla E., 44½
McPherson, Mrs., 102

Mabbett, Ann H., 44½
*Mabbett, Elizabeth T., 45
*Mabbett, Mr. John, 45
Mabbett, Sarah T., 44½
Macy, Cornelia T., 153
Macy, Mrs. Eliza L., 153
*Macy, George Trimble, 152½
*Macy, Mary J., 153
Macy, Josiah, Jr., 153
Macy, Josiah G., 54
Macy, Silvanus J., 152½
Macy, William H., 153
*Macy William H., Jr., 152½
*Malcomson, John, 84
Malcomson, Mr. Joseph, 31
Malcomson, Mrs. Joseph, 31
Marshall, Mrs. Sarah H., 61
Martin, George, 115
Mason, Miss Hannah, 11
Massey, Charles, Jr., 159
Massey, R. V., 171
Massey, Miss Susan, 171
Mather, Mrs. Ann W., 164½
*Mather, Catherine M., 164½
Maxfield, Joseph, 140

*Silhouette missing

The names of the sitters and the pages correspond to the numbers Edouart used in the Quaker Duplicate Book.

Maylor, James, 204½
Mayfield, John, 1
Medcalfe, William M., 101
*Metford, Cornelia, 48
Metford, Miss Eleanor, 50
Metford, Mrs. Francis (Phebe), 50
*Metford, Francis, 49
Metford, Henry, 50½
*Metford, Joseph Sr., 50
*Metford, Joseph Sr., 48
*Metford, Samuel, 49
*Metford, Thomas Beaven, Jr., 48
Minster, Emily, 169
Minster, Mr. George, 169
Minster, Mrs. George, 169
Minister, Joseph Lea, 169
Mitchell, Mrs. Eunice, 78½
Moore, Catherine, 164
Moore, John R., 164½
Moore, Mrs. William T. & Infant, 61
Morris, Mrs. Elizabeth, 131½
Morris, Theodore (Israel), 131½
Morris, Miss Mary E., 126
Morris, Paschall, 143
Morton, Samuel C., 55
Morton, Dr. Samuel George, 132½
Mott, Ann Elizabeth, 67
*Mott, Harriet S., 68
Mott, Mr. James, 116
Mott, Mrs. James, 116
Mott, Miss Louisa, 67
Mott, Samuel T., Jr., 67
Mott, Samuel T., Sr. (2 poses), 67
*Mott, Samuel T., Sr., 66½
*Mott, William T., Jr., 68

Neall, Hannah M., 66
Newbold, Miss Charlotte, 154
Newbold, Mrs. E. P., 154
Newbold, Mrs. E. P.'s
　unnamed sister, 154
Newbold, William F., 154
Newlin, Mr. Thomas S., 141
*Newlin, Mrs. Thomas S., 141
Nicholson, Mrs. Fletcher, 20
Nicholson, James, 22½ A
*Nicholson, Joshua Clibborn, 136½
*Nicholson, Mrs. M., 136½
*Nicholson, Meadows T., 136½
Nicholson, Mrs. William, 22½ A
Norris, Lloyd, 101
Nutter, Miss Amelia, 22
Nutter, Benjamin, 22½ A
Nutter, Mrs. Hannah, 22
Nutter, Samuel, 22½ A
Nutter, Mr. William, 22
Nutter, Mrs. William, 22

O'Brien, Maria W., 75
*Opie, Amelia, 1½

*Palmer, Charles, 107
Palmer, Mr. Edward, 107
Palmer, Miss Fanny, 107
Palmer, Henry, 106
Palmer, Mr. Jonathan, Jr., 106
Palmer, Miss Sarah, 106
Palmer, Mrs. Sarah H., 106
Parke, Miss Hannah, 105
Parke, Mr. James P., 105
Parrish, Dr. Joseph, 162
*Parsons, Elizabeth J., 69
Parsons, Mr. James B., 69

*Parsons, Mrs. James B., 69
*Parsons, John Brown, 69
*Parsons, Samuel, Sr., 69
Parsons, Samuel B., Jr., (2 poses), 68½
Parsons, Samuel B., Sr., 68½
*Paschall, Thomas, 206
*Paxton, Samuel C., 68
*Pearsall, Mr. Robert, 131
Pearsall, Mrs. Robert, 131
Pearson, James, Esquire, 25
Pease, Joseph, Esquire (2 poses), 3
Pease, Miss, 3
*Pemberton, James, 205
*Pemberton, John, 205
Pennock, Caroline, 149
Pennock, Miss Isabella L., 149
Pennock, Sarah, 149
Pennock, Mrs. Sarah, 149
Perry, Charles, 92
Perry, Miss Elizabeth, 92
Perry, Thomas, 92
*Phelps, Mary Jane, 29
Pim, Edward, 34
Pim, Mrs. Edward, 34
Pim, Master Edward Wakefield, 34
Pim, George, Esquire, 14
*Pim, George C., 29
*Pim, Mrs. George C., 29
Pim, Miss Hannah, 28
Pim, Mrs. Hannah, 28
*Pim, John, Sr., Esquire, 30
Pim, John, Esquire, 14
*Pim, Marguerite, 30
*Pim, Mary, 29
Pim, Miss Mary Strangman, 30
Pim, Mr. Richard, Esquire, 12
Pim, Mrs. Richard, 12
Pim, Miss Ruth, 12
*Pim, Samuel, 30
Pim, Tobias, 28
*Pleasant, Mary, 206
*Pleasant, Samuel, 206
*Poultney, Benjamin, 95
*Pratt, M. C., 97
Pratt, Micajah C., 97
Price, Mr. Eli, 151
Price, Mrs. Eli K., 151
Price, Mrs. Lydia W., 104
Price, Mary Ferris, 151
Price, Mr. Philip M., 150½
Price, Mrs. Philip M., 150½
Price, Sibbylla E., 151
Proud, Robert, 204½
Pugh, Miss Sarah, 103
Pumphrey, Stanley, Esquire, 1

*Rabb, Christine, 56½ B
*Randolph, Edward, Jr., 120
*Randolph, George, 120
*Randolph, George F. (2 poses), 121
*Randolph, Miss Hannah F., 121
Randolph, Miss Jane F., 121
*Randolph, Nathaniel, 120
*Randolph, Richard, 120
Rawle, William, 204
Reynolds, Mrs. Hannah, 4
Reynolds, Richard, 4
Rhoads, Sarah, 205
*Richardson, Mr. James, 13
Ridgway, J., 100
*Ridgway, Mary, 205
Ring, Mrs. George, 66½
*Rively, Sarah C., 66

Robeson, Mrs. Elizabeth, 163
Robeson, Mr. Jonathan, 164
Robeson, Sarah, 163
Robeson, William R., 169
Robinson, Miss Eliza, 13
Robinson, Miss Mary, 11
Robinson, Mr. Joseph, 13
Robinson, Mrs. Joseph, 13
Robinson, Master M., 13
Robinson, Mr. William, 11
Russell, Mrs. Benjamin, 87

*Sansom, Miss Hannah, 147
*Sansom, Mrs. Susan, 147
Savery, William, 205
Scattergood, Thomas, 204
Sharpless, Anna, 88
Sharpless, Charles L., 88
Sharpless, Henry H. G., 88
Sharpless, Mrs. Sarah D., 88
Shillitoe, Miss M. A., 27
Shillitoe, Thomas, 205
*Shillitoe, Mrs. Thomas, 27
*Shillitoe, William Man, Jr., 27
*Shoemaker, Samuel, 204½
*Sholl, John, 82
Shorthouse, William, Esquire, 20
Shorthouse, Mrs. William, 20
Shotwell, Miss Anna, 40
Shotwell, Miss Mary, 40
*Shotwell, Mrs. Sarah, 40
*Shotwell, Mr., 40
Shotwell, Mr. William, 41
Shotwell, Mrs. William, 41
Simmons, Thomas, 11
Smart, Miss Mary, 90
Smith, Albanus, 130½
*Smith, Alfred, 73
Smith, Mrs. Alfred C., 73
Smith, Mr. Edmund Burk, 167
Smith, Mrs. Edmund Burk, 167
*Smith, Horace John, 130½
Smith, Lloyd P., 130½
*Smith, Oscar Bloodgood, 73
*Smith, Richard, 206
Smith, Richard, 204½
Smith, Robert P., 130½
Smith, Miss Sally F., 114
Smith, Mrs. Sarah, 22½ A
Smith, Mrs. Susanna R., 65
Smith, Miss W., 10
Southall, Miss Anna Marie, 24
Southall, Miss Ellen, 24
Southall, Miss Isabel, 24
Southall, Miss Marguerite, 24
Spriggs, Mr. William, 10
Spriggs, Mrs. William, 10
Stabler, Edward H., 100
*Stokes, Mary, 133
Strangman, Edward, 14

Tappan, Israel W., 82
Tatham, Benjamin, Jr., 126
Tatham, George N., 126
Tatham, Mr. Henry B., 126
Tatham, Mrs. Henry B., 126
*Tatnall, Edward, 95
Taylor, Miss Emma Louisa, 127
Taylor, Mr. F., 127
Taylor, Miss Sarah, 127
Taylor, Thomas N., 127
Thomas, Evan, 100
Thomas, Mr. P. E., 100

*Silhouette missing

The names of the sitters and the pages correspond to the numbers Edouart used in the Quaker Duplicate Book.

Thompson, Mrs. Lydia P., 143
Thruston, William R., Jr., 92
Thurston, Joseph D., 54
*Titus, P. H., 87
Todhunter, John, Esquire, 11
Trimble, Daniel, 60
*Trimble, Mrs. Daniel, 60
Trimble, Miss Mary, 60, *60½
Truman, Mr. George, 141
Truman, Mrs. George (Catherine), 141
Tucker, Mrs. Hanson, 46
Tyson, Samuel E., M.D., 101
Tyson, William, 101

Underhill, Mr. Abraham S., 76
Underhill, Alice L., 76½
Underhill, Miss Anna, 76
*Underhill, Miss Elizabeth, 76½
Underhill, Miss Hannah, 76
*Underhill, Rebecca F., 85
Underhill, Miss Sarah, 76
Unidentified lady (bust), 175
*Vaux, Annie, 146
*Vaux, Eliza H., 146
*Vaux, Elizabeth, 146
*Vaux, Emilie, 146
Vaux, Miss Frances, 146½
Vaux, George, 146½
*Vaux, Miss Hannah S., 146½
*Vaux, Miss Mary Emlen, 146½
*Vaux, William S., 146

Wakefield, Elizabeth, 15
Wakefield, Miss Isabella N., 15
Wakefield, Mrs. Jane, 15
*Wakefield, John B., 35
*Wakefield, Mrs. John B., 34½, 35
Wakefield, Thomas C., Esq., 15, 34½
*Walker, John B., 79
Walker, John J., 117
Walker, Lewis, 155
Walker, Mrs. Martha W., 155
*Walker, Richard L., 79
*Walker, Robert, 79
*Walker, Mr. Robert J., 79
*Walker, Mrs. Robert J. (Hannah), 79
*Walker, Thomas, 79
*Waln, Nicholas, 205
Warder, Miss Ann, 113
Warder, Miss Eleonor H., 112

Warder, Hannah, 114
Warder, Henrietta, 112
Warder, John H., 112
Warder, William G., 112
*Warner, George, 206
Warner, Mr. Joseph, 173
Warner, Mrs. Joseph (Lydia), 173
Warner, Miers F., 173
Warner, Redwood, 173
Warner, Miss Sally, 173
Waterbury, Lawrence, 83
Waterhouse, Theodore, 1
Watts, Hannah G., 89
*Webb, Anna, 32½
Webb, Miss Charlotte, 32
Webb, Mrs. Maria, 32½
Webb, Wilhelmina, 32, 32½
Webb, William, Esquire, 32
Webb, Master William Henry, 32
*Welding, Watson J., 97
Wetherill, E. K. K., 144
Wetherill, John M., 144½
Wetherill, John Price, 144
Wetherill, Joseph B., 144½
Wetherill, Rachel, 144
Wetherill, Miss Rachel, 145
Wetherill, Samuel, 145
Wetherill, Dr. William, 145
Wetherill, Mrs. William, 145
*Wharton, Charles W., 152
*Wharton, Deborah F., 152
Wharton, Miss Hannah, 42
Wharton, Rodman, 152
Wharton, William, 152
*Wharton, William, Jr., 152
*Wheeler, Daniel, 205
White, Miles, 98
*White, Phebe C., 64
White, Robert, Jr., 64
Williams, Miss Anna R., 88½
Williams, Daniel, Esquire, 204½
Willmore, Benjamin, 1
Willis, Mrs. Elizabeth V., 81
*Willis, Mr. J. R., 81
*Willis, Mrs. J. R., 81
*Willis, Master, 81
Willson, William, 204½
Wistar, Mrs. Annabella C., 103
*Wistar, B. Wyatt, 103
Wistar, Charles J., 105

Wistar, Mr. R., 160
Wistar, Mrs. R., 160
Wistar, Mrs. R. L., 160½
Wistar, Richard, 160½
Wistar, Miss Sarah, 160
Wood, Mrs. C. H., 124
Wood, Caroline, 123
Wood, Charles S., 122
Wood, Mrs. Charles S., 122
Wood, Edward Randolph, 123
Wood, Miss Elizabeth, 122
Wood, Dr. George B., 124
Wood, G. Randolph, 122
Wood, Miss Hannah, 122
Wood, Mrs. Hannah D., 124
Wood, Mary, 123
Wood, Richard D., 123
Wood, Mrs. Richard D., 123
Wood, Master Richard D., 123
Wood, Infant, 123
Woodward, Miss Elizabeth, 71
*Woodward, John D., 70
*Woodward, Thomas, Jr., 70
*Woodward, Thomas, Sr., 70
Woodward, Mrs. Thomas, 71
Wright, Mr. Edward N., 89
*Wright, George A., 55
Wright, Miss Hannah, 109
Wright, Isaac N., 54
*Wright, John Wandesford, 52
Wright, John W., 55
*Wright, Jordon, 72
Wright, Peter I., 107
Wright, Richard, 55

Yardley, Henry Albert, 109
Yardley, Sarah S., 109
Yardley, William L., 109
*Yarnall, Charles, 132
*Yarnall, Ellis, Junior, 82, 132
*Yarnall, Mrs. Emma C., 132
Yarrow, John, 115
*Yates, Elizabeth, 48
Yerbury, Miss, 2
Youle, Miss Josephine S., 111

*Zane, Isaac, 206
Zell, Hannah, 142

*Silhouette missing

The names of the sitters and the pages correspond to the numbers Edouart used in the Quaker Duplicate Book.

Mr. James Mott
Mrs. James ("Lucretia") Mott
(actual size)

The leading woman abolitionist in the United States was this determined Quaker lady named Lucretia Mott. Mr. and Mrs. Mott's silhouettes were cut in Philadelphia on October 21, 1842. (p. 116 in the folio)

Framed and Finished

The following framed and finished groupings are the originals that Edouart sold to his patrons. The backgrounds were custom designed and the individual silhouettes were pasted in place. This Quaker duplicate album contains the mirror images of these sitters, cut at the same time from folded paper. (Edouart explains this practice on page 13.)

*Edouart records an American interior furnished in the Empire style as a background to four generations (duplicates on page 60, 60½, 61)— Winterthur Collection, Inc.: Left to right—Mrs. Hannah Hawxhurst, Mary Trimble, *Mrs. Daniel Trimble, Daniel Trimble, Mrs. William T. Moore, Infant Moore, Mrs. Sarah Marshall. (*silhouette missing from duplicate folio)*

The Vaux Family (duplicates on pages 146, 146½)—private collection: Left to right—Mary Emlen Vaux, Hannah S. Vaux, Susan Vaux Cresson, Annie Vaux, Eliza Vaux, Emilie Vaux, Frances Vaux, William Vaux, Elizabeth Vaux, George Vaux.

*The Robeson and Lea Families (duplicates on pages 163, 164, 165)—private collection: Left to right—Mary Bensell, Mrs. Elizabeth Robeson, Catherine Moore, Jonathan Robeson, *Sarah Robeson, Joseph Lea, Sr., (framed silhouette not identified).*

*The Underhill Family (duplicates on pages 176, 176½)–private collection:
Left to right–Hannah Underhill, Anna Underhill, Abraham S. Underhill,
Sarah Underhill, *missing sitter.*

The Lea Family taken at "Milverton" (duplicates on paper 165, 166, 167)–private collection: Left to right–Joseph Lea, Sr., Joseph Lea, Jr., Frances Lea, Sarah Lea, Anna R. Lea, Elizabeth Lea, Ellenor R. Lea, Martha Lea, Jane P. Lea, Catherine Lea, Mrs. Joseph Lea, Sr.

Thomas Cope (duplicate missing page 133)—private collection.

*The Lea and Minster Families (duplicates on pages 168, 169, 170)— private collection: Left to right—Joseph Tatnall Lea, Robeson Lea, Ellen H. Lea, Richard M. Lea, Thomas T. Lea, (baby on pillow) Thomas T. Lea, Jr., Sally A. Lea, Mrs. Robeson Lea, Mary C. Lea, *Missing sitter, Mrs. Frances Lea, George Minster, (baby) Emily Minster, (baby on pillow) Joseph Lea Minster, Mrs.George Minster, bust silhouettes Mrs. & Mr. Joseph Tatnall:*

More of Edouart's framed and finished Quaker groups from these duplicates must exist. If you know of one or of a Quaker family album of silhouettes, please write: Helen and Nel Laughon, 8106 Three Chopt Road, Richmond, Virginia 23229.

117

Lucy Clarke
(actual size)

This lady is found cutting an unknown profile on page 19 in the British section, cut prior to Edouart's trip to America.

Acknowledgements

Chasing Edouart's Quaker shadows, researching their genealogy, and discovering the contributions of each sitter was a stimulating experience. The silence of this assemblage was broken by the discovery of this folio.

We extend special thanks to the staff of the Friends Historical Library, of Swarthmore College, Swarthmore, Pennsylvania. They offered us invaluable advice throughout the research and writing of the book. They were tireless in sharing information and having the willingness to let us publish this collection: J. William Frost, Albert W. Fowler, Jane M. Thorson, Nancy Speers, Ramsay Turberg, and Kazue Oye.

Our sincere thanks also go to the many friends, collectors, dealers, and scholars who shared with us their expertise, enthusiasm, hospitality, and collections: Shelley Aagesen, Ann Bahar, Marian Carson, Mona Dearborn, Sarah Shields Driggs, Allison M. Eckardt, Josephine Elliott, John Field, Frances Fugate, Emerson Greenaway, Kate Gregory, Eleanor H. Gustafson, W. L. Guyton, Virginius C. Hall, Patricia T. Herr, Bernard Jackson, Christopher N. Jackson, Ron Jennings, Hannah London, Barbara Luck, Alfred Mayor, James McCann, Ellen Miles, W. Donald Rhinesmith, Beatrix Rumford, Anna Rutledge, Sandy Ruzak, John and Emily Salmon, Samuel Shipley, Susan B. Swann, Jessica Travis, Ross Urquhart, George Vaux, and Carolyn J. Weekley.

Many institutions were involved in our search: The Abby Aldrich Rockefeller Folk Art Center, Williamsburg, Virginia; The Art Institute of Chicago, Chicago, Illinois; Bryn Mawr College, Bryn Mawr, Pennsylvania; The Charleston Museum, Charleston, South Carolina; Haverford College, Haverford, Pennsylvania; Historic New Orleans Collection, New Orleans, Louisiana; Kentucky Historical Society, Frankfort, Kentucky; The Library of Congress, Washington, D.C.; The Library Company, Philadelphia, Pennsylvania; Massachusetts Historical Society, Boston Massachusetts; The Metropolitan Museum of Art, New York, New York; Museum of Early Southern Decorative Arts, Winston-Salem, North Carolina; The National Portrait Gallery, Washington, D.C., The New-York Historical Society, New York, New York; Rare Books, New York Public Library, New York, New York; The Historical Society of Pennsylvania, Philadelphia, Pennsylvania; Pendle Hill, Wallingford, Pennsylvania; Portland Museum of Art, Portland Maine; Historical Society of Saratoga Springs, Saratoga Springs, New York; Transylvania College, Lexington, Kentucky; The Valentine Museum, Richmond, Virginia; Virginia Historical Society, Richmond, Virginia; The Winterthur Museum, Inc., Winterthur, Delaware.

Thanks to our friends at these institutions in Great Britain visited on the trail of Edouart: Friends House, London; The National Portrait Gallery, London; The National Portrait Gallery of Scotland, Edinburgh, Scotland; Victoria and Albert Museum, London. Individual thanks to Richard Allen, Sotheby Parke Bernet and Company, London; Ian Cross, Silhouette Club, Dummer, England; Percy Higgs, E. Grosvenor Paine, J. A. Pollak, and Julius Smit, of London.

Our appreciation is extended to the Friends Meeting Houses in Lincoln, Virginia; Philadelphia, Pennsylvania; Richmond, Virginia; and London that we attended to feel the "Inner Light."

Our heartfelt thanks to the now-deceased British scholars: Andrew Tuer, pioneer critic who dreamed of finding the lost folios; Mrs. Emily Nevill Jackson for the discovery of many of the surviving duplicate folios, her research, and publications; John Woodiwiss, Desmond Coke, and Sue McKechnie for their wonderful books on British silhouettes with further insights into Edouart's British cuttings. And admiration to the American writers and collectors now deceased: Alice Van Leer Carrick, Helen McCormack, Glenn Tilley Morse, Mary Martin, Arthur S. Vernay, Ethel S. Bolton, and Andrew Oliver for their tracing the American tour of this prolific profile artist.

Special love and thanks to Wendell Garrett for his encouragement and his gift with the written word; Joan Kendall at Hatfield House, Hatfield, Hertfordshire, England, for her knowledge of Quaker costumes; and Eleanore Price Mather, now deceased, for her love of the Quakers, their history, and their impact on America.

Miss Catherine M. Lea
Miss Elizabeth Lea
(actual size)

These two silhouettes have white lines added for a more life-like appearance. Edouart had said he did not like any additions to the black silhouette in his TREATISE of 1835. The popularity of the Daguerrotype caused this major alteration in style. To students of his work, this was a surprise that this album disclosed. The Leas were cut in 1842 and are on page 165.

Select Bibliography

Books and Exhibition Catalogs

Bolton, Ethel Stanwood. *Wax Portraits and Silhouettes.* Boston: The Massachusetts Society of the Colonial Dames of America, 1914.

Brinton, Anna Cox. *Quaker Profiles.* Wallingford, Pa.: Pendle Hill Publications, 1964.

Carrick, Alice Van Leer. *Shades of Our Ancestors: American Profiles and Profilists.* Boston: Little, Brown, and Company, 1928.

Edouart, Monsieur. *A Treatise on Silhouette Likeness.* London: Longman and Company, 1835.

Encyclopedia of American Biography. Edited by William Richard Cutter. 54 vols. New York: American Historical Society, 1916–1933.

Frost, Jerry William. *The Quaker Family in Colonial America, a portrait of the Society of Friends.* New York: St. Martin's Press, 1973.

Gummere, Amelia M. *The Quaker: A Study in Costume.* Philadelphia: Ferris and Leach, 1901.

Hinshaw, William Wade. *The Encyclopedia of American Quaker Genealogy.* 6 vols. Ann Arbor, Mich.: Edwards Brothers, Inc., 1938.

Jackson, E. Nevill. *The History of Silhouette.* London: Connoisseur, 1911.

_____. *Silhouettes: A History and Dictionary of Artists.* New York: Dover Publications, 1981.

_____. *Silhouette Notes and Dictionary.* New York: Charles Scribner's Sons, 1938. Reprint ed. New York: Dover Publications, 1981.

Jackson, F. Nevill. *Ancestors in Silhouette, Cut by August Edouart.* London and New York: Lane, 1921.

_____. *Catalogue of 3,800 Named and Dated American Silhouette Portraits by August Edouart, 1789–1861.* London, n.d.

_____. *Catalogue of 5,200 Named and Dated English Silhouette Portraits by August Edouart, 1789–1861.* London: Walbrook, 1911.

_____. *Catalogue and Supplement of 5,800 Named and Dated Silhouette Portraits by August Edouart, 1789–1861.* London: n.p., n.d.

Lamb, Charles. *The Essays of Elia and the Last Essays of Elia.* London: Oxford University Press, 1820–1833.

Lavater, John Casper. *Essays on Physiognomy.* (Translated into English by Thomas Holcroft.) London: Whittingham, 1804.

McKechnie, Sue. *British Silhouette Artists and Their Work, 1760–1860.* London: Sotheby Parke Bernet, 1978.

Mayo, Abigail DeHart. *An American Lady in Paris, 1828–1829.* Edited by Mary Mayo Crenshaw. Boston and New York: Houghton Mifflin Company, 1927.

Mégroz, R. L. *Profile Art Through the Ages.* London: The Art Trade Press, Ltd., 1948.

Oliver, Andrew. *Auguste Edouart's Silhouettes of Eminent Americans, 1839–1844.* Charlottesville, Va.: University Press of Virginia, 1977.

Roe, F. Gordon. *Women in Profile: A Study in Silhouette.* London: John Baker, 1970.

Rutledge, Anna Wells. *Artists in the Life of Charleston.* Columbia: University of South Carolina Press, 1980. First Edition in Philadelphia, Pa. *Transactions of the American Philosophical Society,* New Series, volume 39, part 2, 1949.

Vernay, Arthur S. *A Catalogue of Silhouettes by August Edouart.* New York: privately printed, 1913.

_____. *The Collection of American Silhouette Portraits Cut by August Edouart.* New York: n.p., 1913.

Wilson, James Grant, and Fiske, John, eds. *Appleton's Cyclopedia of American Biography.* 6 vols. New York: D. Appleton and Company, 1887.

Wilson, Robert. *Philadelphia Quaker, 1681–1981.* Philadelphia: Philadelphia Yearly Meeting of the Religious Society of Friends, 1981.

Articles in Journals and Magazines

"Auguste Edouart's Silhouettes of Federal America, 1839–1849." *American Antiques* (April 1978): 20–27.

Bahar, Ann. "Auguste Edouart: Adventure in Shadow." *Hobbies* (November 1985): 68–72.

Dodge, Wendell Phillips. "The Silhouette: Beginning of Portrait Art," *Craftsman* (January 1914): 324–329.

Helfer, Harold. "Shades of the Past." *Aloft* (1977): 64–68.

Laughon, Helen and Nel. "A newly identified Edouart folio." *The Magazine Antiques* (December 1984): 1446–1450.

_____. "August Edouart: A Quaker Album of American and English Duplicate Silhouettes, 1827–1845." *The Pennsylvania Magazine of History and Biography* 109 (July 1985): 387–398.

Moss, Sanford A. "Silhouettes by Edouart." *The Magazine Antiques* (October 1941): 227–228.

Ritchan. "Hair Portraiture." *The Connoisseur* (December 1932): 392–393.

Rogers, Meyric. "Shadows of the 1840's." *American Collector* (April 1943): 6–7.

Snow, Richard. "The Art of the Silhouette." *Americana* (November 1973): 7–11.

Sommer, Frank H., III. "Joseph Sansom: Recorder of 'Remarkable Persons.' " *Winterthur* (Spring 1987): 14.

Tolles, Frederick B. "Quaker Profiles at Swarthmore." *Friends Intelligencer* (September 28, 1946): 561–562.

Dog on chair
Sarah Pennock
(actual size)

This trained pet was shaking hands with Sarah for the Pennock family group portrait that was taken in Philadelphia in 1843. The duplicate is on page 149.

Conclusion

Having now brought this little Treatise on Silhouettes to a close—before offering it to the favor of an enlightened Public, I think I may be permitted to express a hope, that it will be received with the same feelings as those which actuated me, while engaged in its composition.

—Treatise, p. 113.

COLOPHON

The text of this book is set in Baskerville. Text paper is 80 lb. Potlatch Karma Natural. Cover is Roxite C. Vellum. Composed by Carter Printing Company and Coghill Composition Company, Richmond, Virginia. Printed and bound by BookCrafters, Chelsea, Michigan. Designed by Geary and Flynn Design, Inc., Richmond, Virginia.

The Bedtime Book of
Dinosaurs
and Other Prehistoric Life

Meet more than **100** creatures
from long ago

Written by: Dr Dean Lomax
Illustrated by: Jean Claude, Kaja Kajfež,
Marc Pattenden, Sara Ugolotti

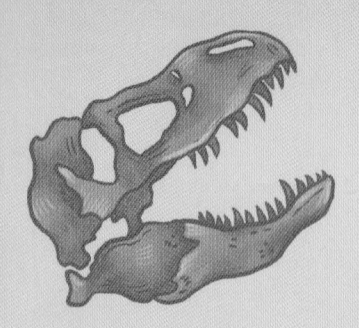

Contents

Tree of life 4
Fossils 6
Changing Earth 8

Paleozoic Era

Charnia 12
Dickinsonia 13
Haikouichthys 14
Elrathia 15
Opabinia 16
Hallucigenia 17
Cambrian seas 18
Didymograptus 20
Astraspis 21
Cooksonia 22
Eurypterus 23
Zenaspis 24
Walliserops 25
Mucrospirifer 26
Attercopus 27
Eusthenopteron 28
Dunkleosteus 29
Devonian swamp 30
Ichthyostega 32
Stethacanthus 33
Calamites 34
Woodocrinus 35
Arthropleura 36
Meganeura 38

Edaphosaurus 39
Dimetrodon 40
Seymouria 41
Scutosaurus 42
Elginia 43

Mesozoic Era

Nothosaurus 46
Stagonolepis 47
Triassic floodplain 48
Shonisaurus 50
Eoraptor 51
Coelophysis 52
Postosuchus 53
Ichthyosaurus 54
Dilophosaurus 56
Heterodontosaurus 57
Megazostrodon 58
Cryolophosaurus 59
Dactylioceras 60
Lepidotes 61
Liopleurodon 62
Cylindroteuthis 63
Yi 64
Mamenchisaurus 65
Stegosaurus 66
Diplodocus 67
Jurassic islands 68
Brachiosaurus 70
Wuerhosaurus 72

Crioceratites	73
Polacanthus	74
Iguanodon	75
Baryonyx	76
Mei	77
Cretaceous forest	78
Pterodaustro	80
Changmiania	82
Archaeanthus	83
Muttaburrasaurus	84
Argentinosaurus	85
Spinosaurus	86
Deinosuchus	87
Maiasaura	88
Euoplocephalus	90
Lambeosaurus	91
Velociraptor	92
Archelon	93
Citipati	94
Albertonectes	95
Einiosaurus	96
Mosasaurus	97
Gallimimus	98
Deinocheirus	99
Indosuchus	100
Quetzalcoatlus	101
Pachycephalosaurus	102
Triceratops	103
Tyrannosaurus	104

Cenozoic Era

Titanoboa	108
Icaronycteris	109
Ambulocetus	110
Banksia archaeocarpa	111
Eosimias	112
Andrewsarchus	113
Basilosaurus	114
Anthropornis	115
Paleogene plains	116
Paraceratherium	118
Palaeocastor	119
Amphicyon	120
Megalodon	121
Chalicotherium	122
Platybelodon	123
Ceratogaulus	124
Macrauchenia	125
Australopithecus	126
Glyptodon	127
Smilodon	128
Thylacoleo	130
Procoptodon	131
Arctodus	132
Mylodon	133
Diprotodon	134
Ancient bison	135
Woolly mammoth	136
Ice Age steppe	138
Glossary	140
Prehistoric A–Z	142
Acknowledgements	144

Mammals
Warm-blooded mammals have **hair** and feed their young on **milk**.

Smilodon

Amphibians
Amphibians are animals that live on **land** and in the **water**.

Seymouria

Invertebrates
These are animals that do not have a **backbone**, such as worms and insects.

Opabinia

Tree of life

The tree of life shows how both living and extinct animals and plants are **connected**. Each branch represents a group of life forms that are **related** to each other.

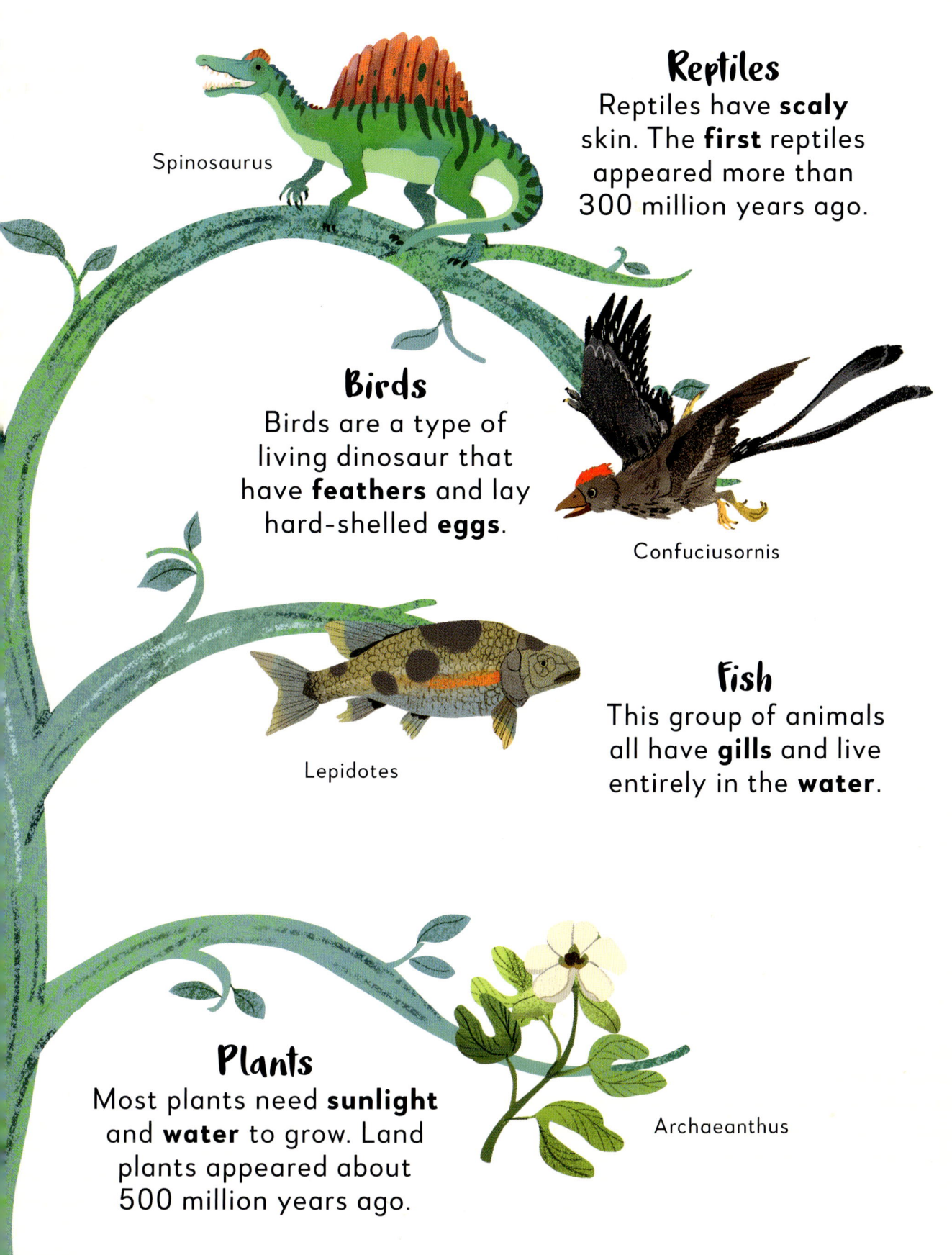

Reptiles
Reptiles have **scaly** skin. The **first** reptiles appeared more than 300 million years ago.

Spinosaurus

Birds
Birds are a type of living dinosaur that have **feathers** and lay hard-shelled **eggs**.

Confuciusornis

Fish
This group of animals all have **gills** and live entirely in the **water**.

Lepidotes

Plants
Most plants need **sunlight** and **water** to grow. Land plants appeared about 500 million years ago.

Archaeanthus

Fossils

Fossils are the remains or traces of ancient life found in **rock**. They show us the **incredible** creatures and plants that once lived on Earth.

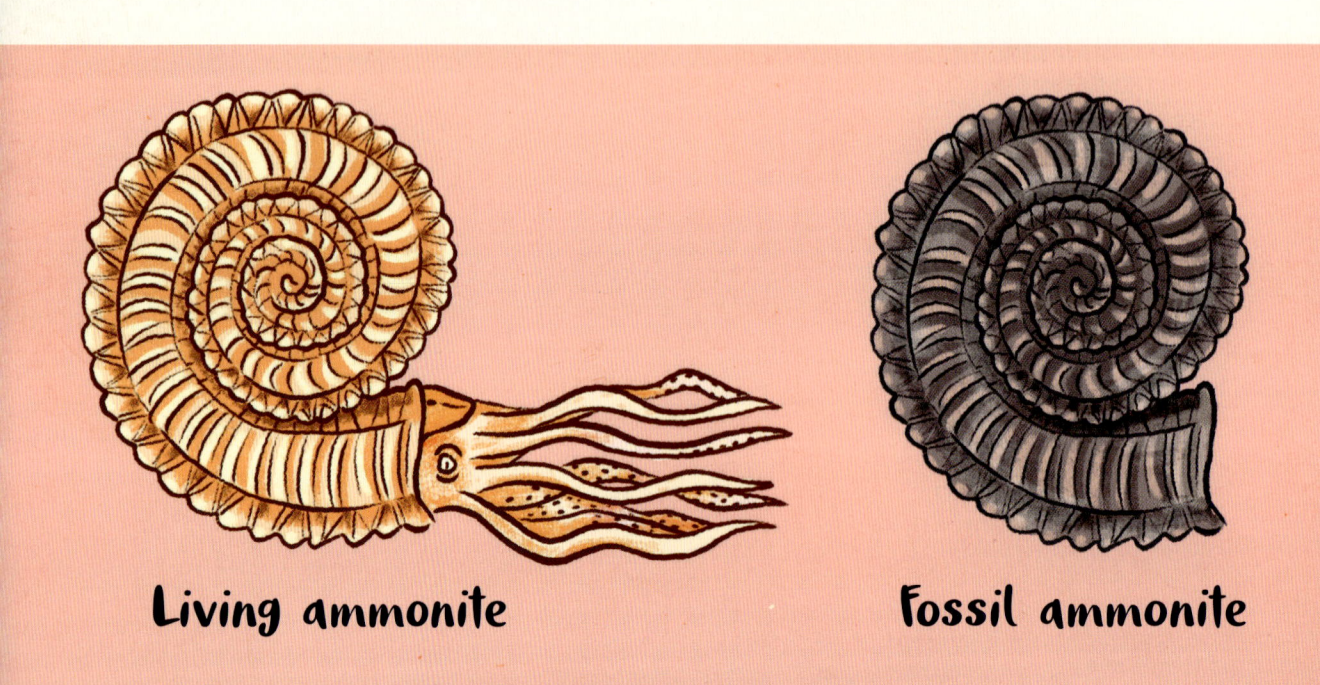

Living ammonite

Fossil ammonite

Animals into fossils

Sometimes after life forms die, they become **buried** in the ground. Over millions of years, their hard parts can transform into rock.

Types of fossil

Body fossils

These are the remains of **parts** of an animal or plant. Examples include bones, teeth, leaves, and shells.

Dinosaur teeth are some of the most common body fossils.

Trace fossils

Trace fossils show us the **behaviours** of prehistoric animals. They include footprints, burrows, and fossilized poo.

Footprints can tell us how fast an animal moved.

Amber

Insects are the most common animals found inside amber.

Creatures can get stuck inside sticky tree **resin**. The resin hardens into amber, making a fossil.

500 million years ago

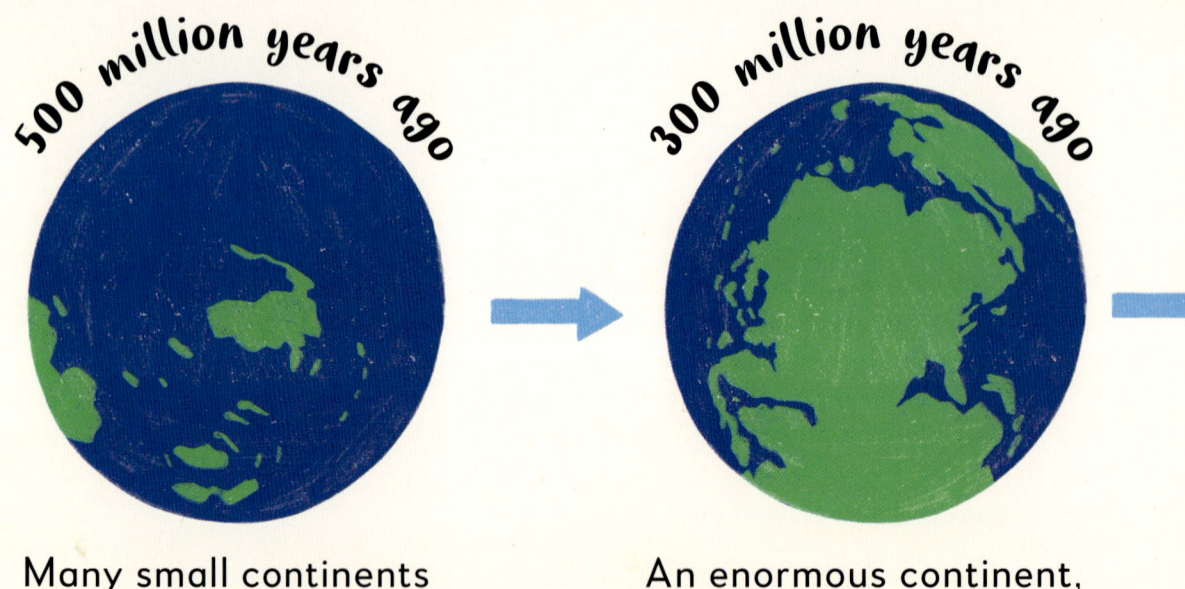

Many small continents and one large continent existed.

300 million years ago

An enormous continent, called Pangea, stretched from north to south.

Changing Earth

The Earth is more than 4 billion years old! Over that time, the chunks of land called **continents** have changed shape and position, and whole oceans have appeared and **disappeared**.

120 million years ago

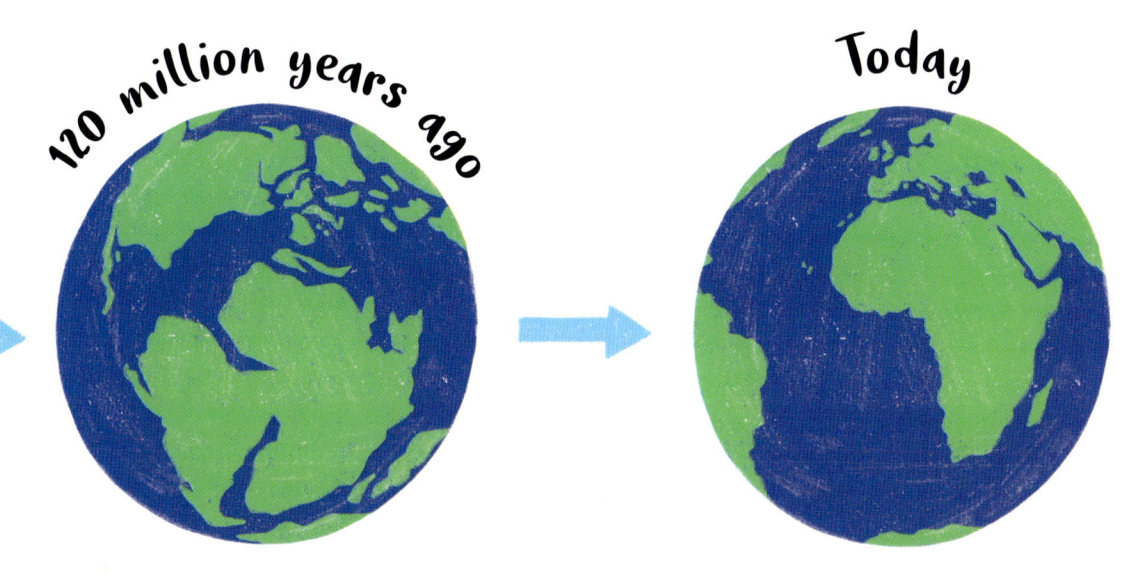

The continents split and pulled apart. They looked more like they do now.

Today

There are seven continents in the world today.

Jigsaw Earth

The Earth's surface is like a giant **puzzle**. The pieces fit together, but they move over time, which causes the land and sea above them to move too.

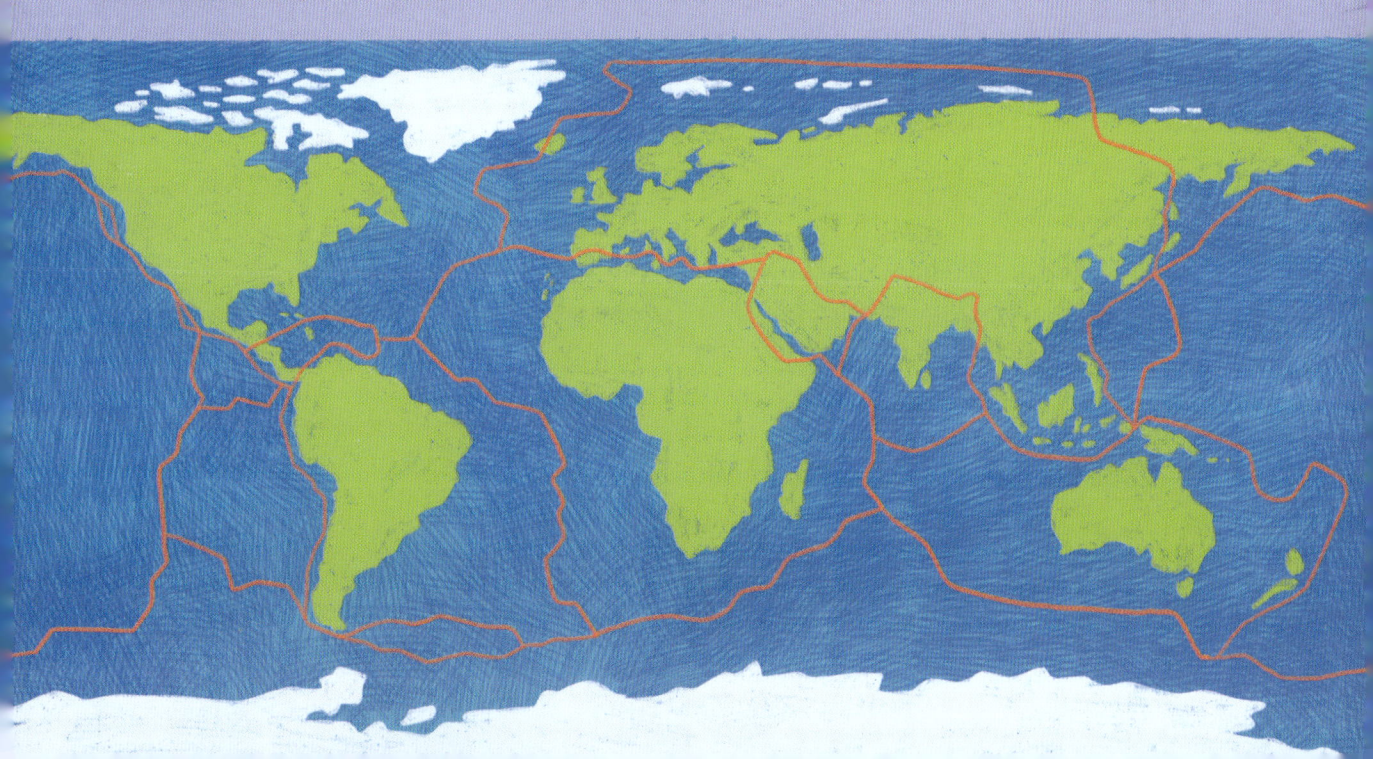

Paleozoic Era

(pay-lee-oh-ZOH-ik EE-ra)

Cambrian Period
541–485 million years ago

The name Paleozoic means "ancient life".

Silurian Period
444–419 million years ago

Ordovician Period
485–444 million years ago

The Paleozoic Era was a long stretch of time, divided up into six shorter **periods**. This era was **bursting** with life. The first animals with backbones appeared in water.

Carboniferous Period
359–299 million years ago

Devonian Period
419–359 million years ago

Permian Period
299–252 million years ago

Mesozoic Era ▶

Before Cambrian

Charnia was one of the first large animals.

Leaf-like shape

Long, flat body

Stem

Charnia

(CHAR-nee-a)

Charnia might look like a plant, but it was actually a type of **animal**. It lived its life anchored to the seafloor more than **500 million** years ago.

Dickinsonia

(dih-kin-SOH-nee-a)

This is one of the **earliest** and most puzzling animals of all. It was a mysterious creature with a squishy body that was flat and round like a **pancake**.

Scientists cannot agree which part of this animal was the **front** and which was the **back**.

A **groove** separated the body into two halves.

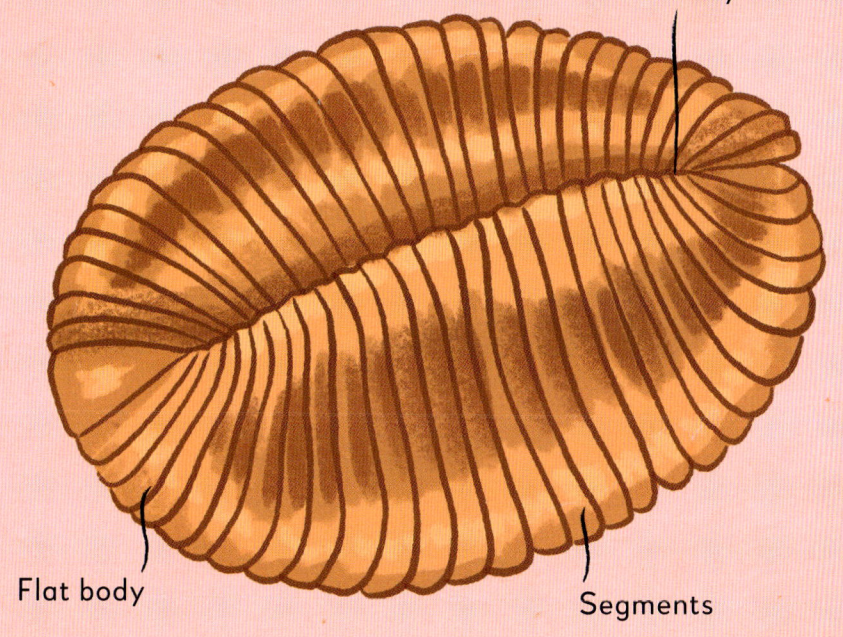

Flat body

Segments

Cambrian

Haikouichthys
(hai-koo-IK-thiss)

Slippery Haikouichthys was among the **first** animals with a backbone. Scientists think it might be one of the **earliest** fish or fish-like animals to have appeared.

Fins

Haikouichthys had two **eyes**, but no jaws or teeth.

Gills were used for breathing underwater.

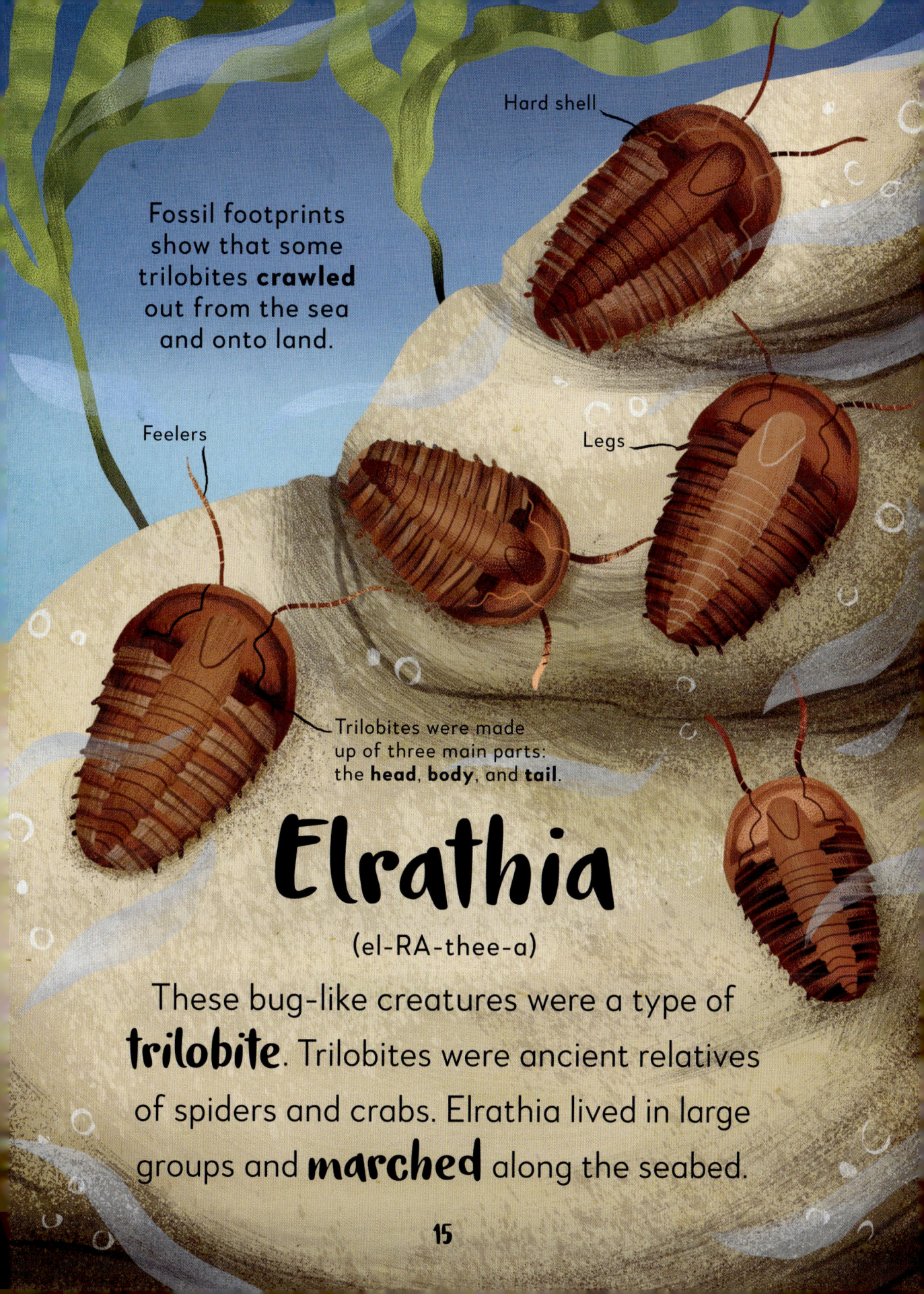

Fossil footprints show that some trilobites **crawled** out from the sea and onto land.

Hard shell

Feelers

Legs

Trilobites were made up of three main parts: the **head**, **body**, and **tail**.

Elrathia

(el-RA-thee-a)

These bug-like creatures were a type of **trilobite**. Trilobites were ancient relatives of spiders and crabs. Elrathia lived in large groups and **marched** along the seabed.

Cambrian

Scientists are still unsure what type of animal Opabinia was.

Five eyes

Opabinia's body was divided into **segments**.

A long, bendy arm on the head had a **claw** for snatching prey.

Opabinia

(oh-pa-BIN-ee-a)

This odd animal had **five** eyes shaped like mushrooms on the top of its head. It swam by **flapping** the bendy sides of its body.

Hallucigenia

(ha-loo-si-JEE-nee-a)

This strange creature looked like a **sausage** with 10 pairs of legs. When it was first found, scientists had it **upside down** and thought its spines were its legs.

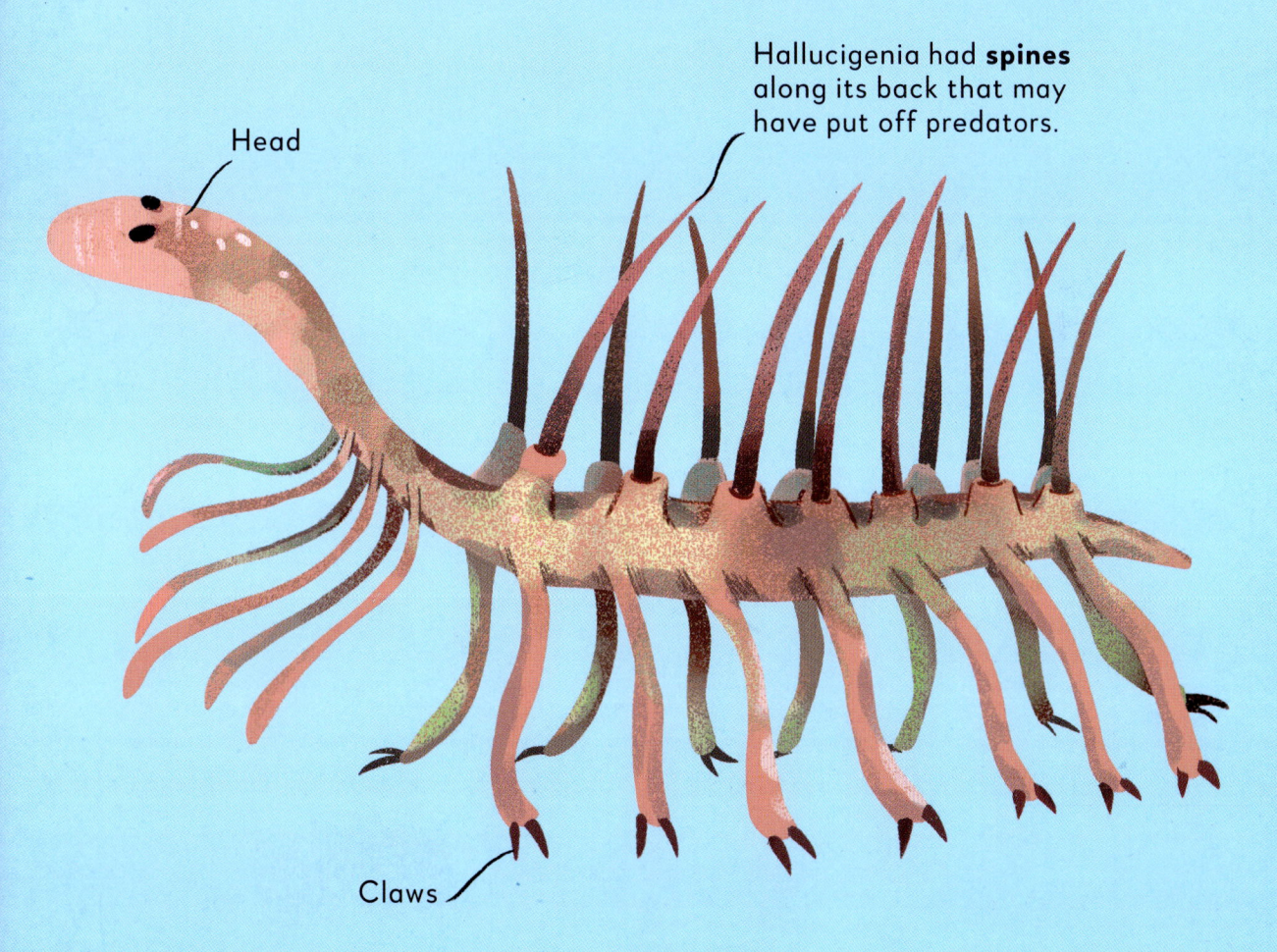

Hallucigenia had **spines** along its back that may have put off predators.

Head

Claws

Cambrian

Cambrian seas

During the Cambrian Period, the sea was filled with **weird** and **wonderful** animals. Many had unusual body shapes and some had hard shells.

This tiny, **crab-like** critter lived near the ocean floor.

Marrella
(ma-RELL-a)

Wiwaxia
(wih-WAKS-ee-a)

Wiwaxia was an animal that had plates of armour and long **spikes** to protect itself.

Anomalocaris
(a-nom-a-loh-KAR-iss)

This strange creature was the top **predator** in Cambrian seas, feasting on lots of other animals.

Pikaia
(pih-KAI-a)

Pikaia looked a bit like a flattened **eel**.

Ottoia was a type of worm that lived inside burrows.

Ottoia's tubular **mouth** was covered in hooks and spines.

Ottoia
(o-TOI-a)

19

Ordovician

These graptolites had two arms that attached at the **top**.

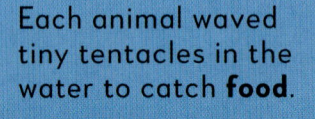

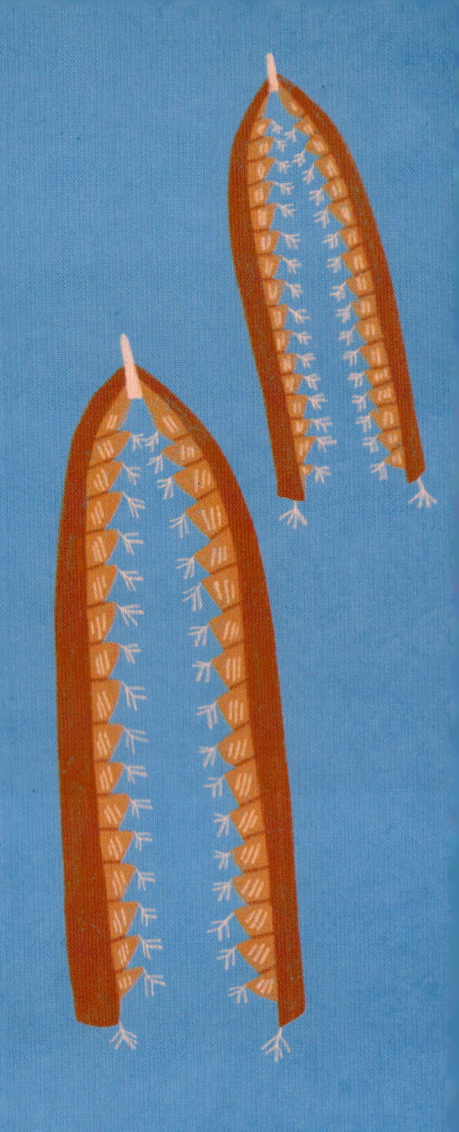

Each animal waved tiny tentacles in the water to catch **food**.

Didymograptus
(did-ee-moh-GRAP-tuss)

This U-shaped sea creature is called a **graptolite**. Its body was created by a team of **tiny** animals that each built one part of its two arms.

Astraspis probably sucked up mud from the seafloor and sieved out tiny animals to **eat**.

Sleek body

Scales

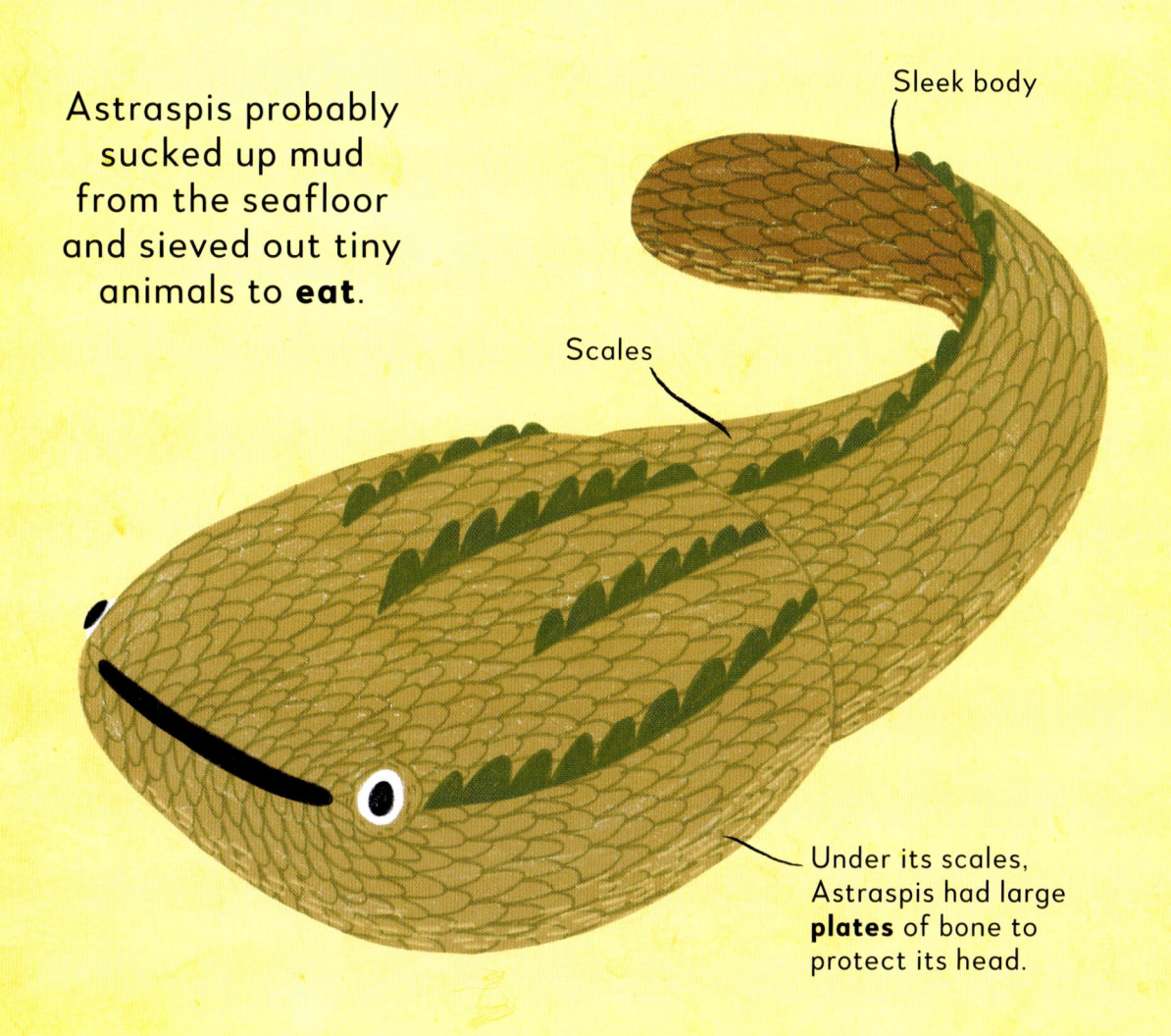

Under its scales, Astraspis had large **plates** of bone to protect its head.

Astraspis

(a-STRA-spiss)

This small fish was covered in tough **scales** for protection against predators. It lived close to the seafloor near the **shore**.

Silurian

Cooksonia

(cuk-SOH-nee-a)

Cooksonia was one of the earliest **plants** to live on **land**, appearing more than 400 million years ago. Unlike plants today, it did not have leaves, flowers, or roots.

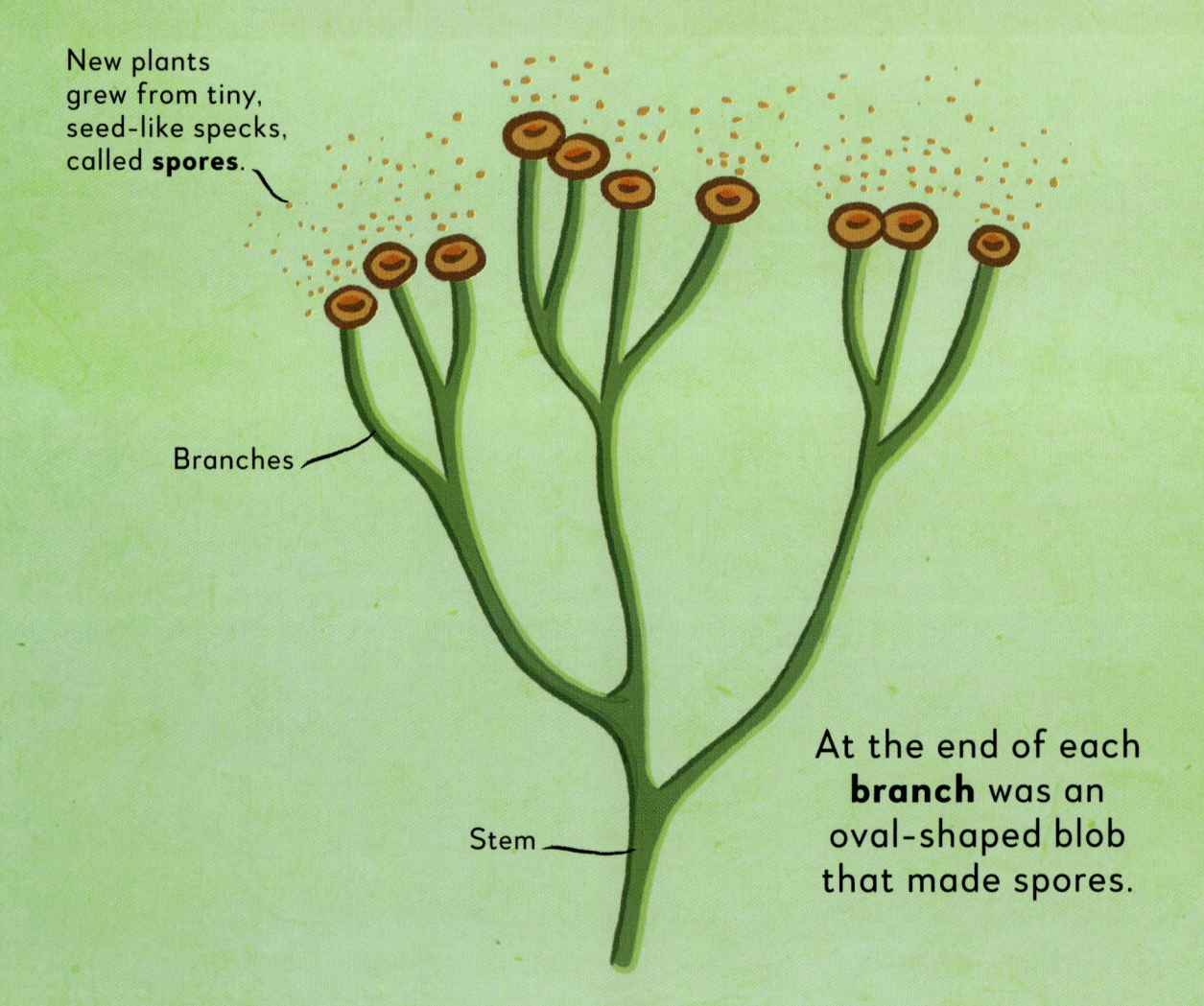

New plants grew from tiny, seed-like specks, called **spores**.

Branches

Stem

At the end of each **branch** was an oval-shaped blob that made spores.

Eurypterus

(yoo-RIP-teh-russ)

Eurypterus was a type of animal known as a **sea scorpion**. These critters were named for their **pointed** tail spikes. Eurypterus used its flat back legs to paddle through the water.

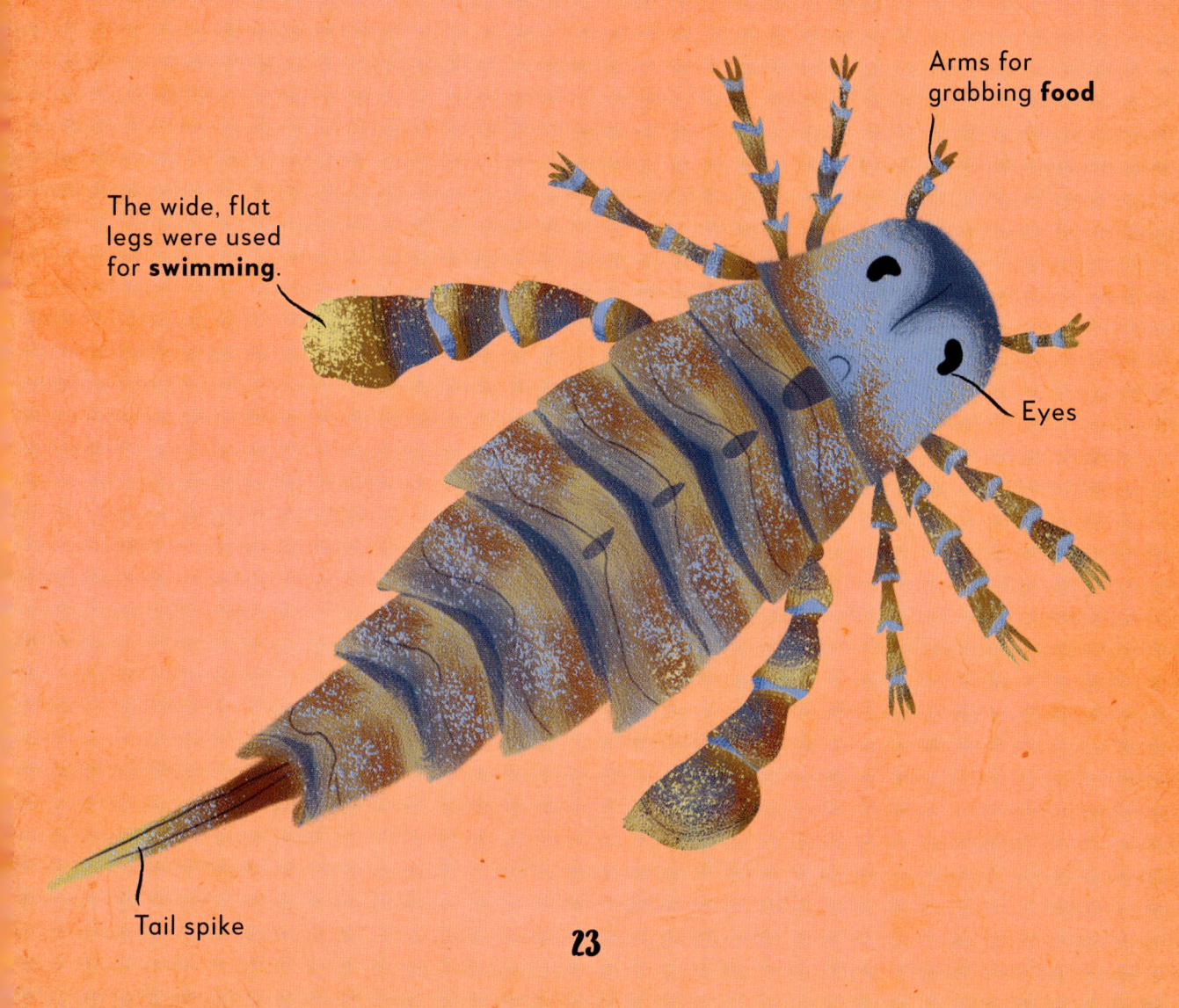

Arms for grabbing **food**

The wide, flat legs were used for **swimming**.

Eyes

Tail spike

Devonian

Zenaspis

(zen-ASP-iss)

This fish didn't have any jaws to bite with, so it had to **slurp** up prey from the seafloor. It had a hard head shield that **protected** it from predators.

Tail

Zenaspis' **mouth** was underneath its head.

Eyes

Head shield

Walliserops may have used the trident on its head to **feel** its way around.

Walliserops had many **spines**. Some even stuck out above its eyes.

Head shield

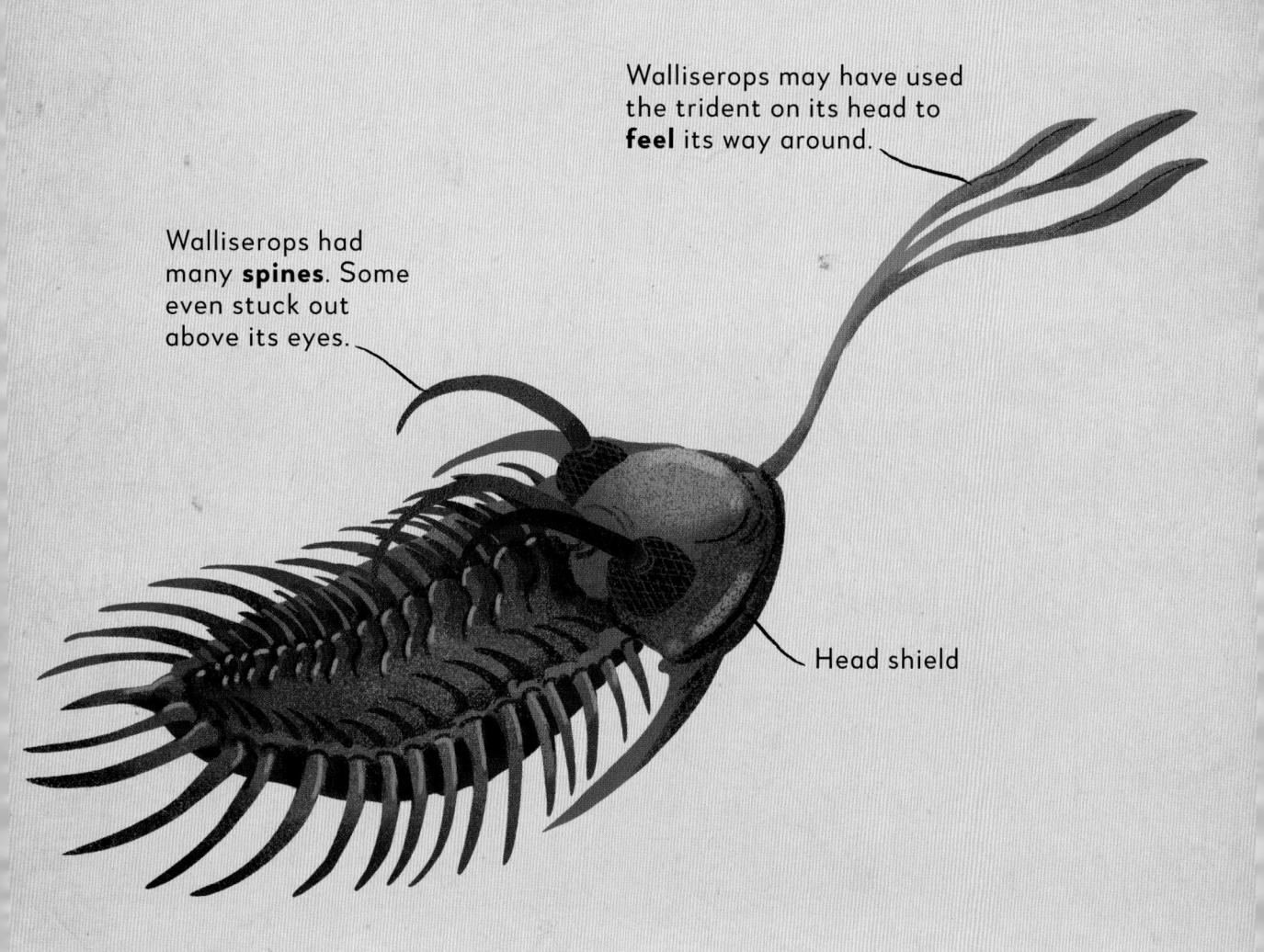

Walliserops

(WALL-ee-seh-rops)

Trilobites, such as Walliserops, were ancient relatives of crabs that looked like underwater woodlice. Walliserops had an unusual **trident** sticking out of its head, which had three points.

25

Devonian

Mucrospirifer lived its life attached to the **seafloor**, catching food with its long tentacles.

Tentacles

Ridges ran along both halves of the shell.

Shell

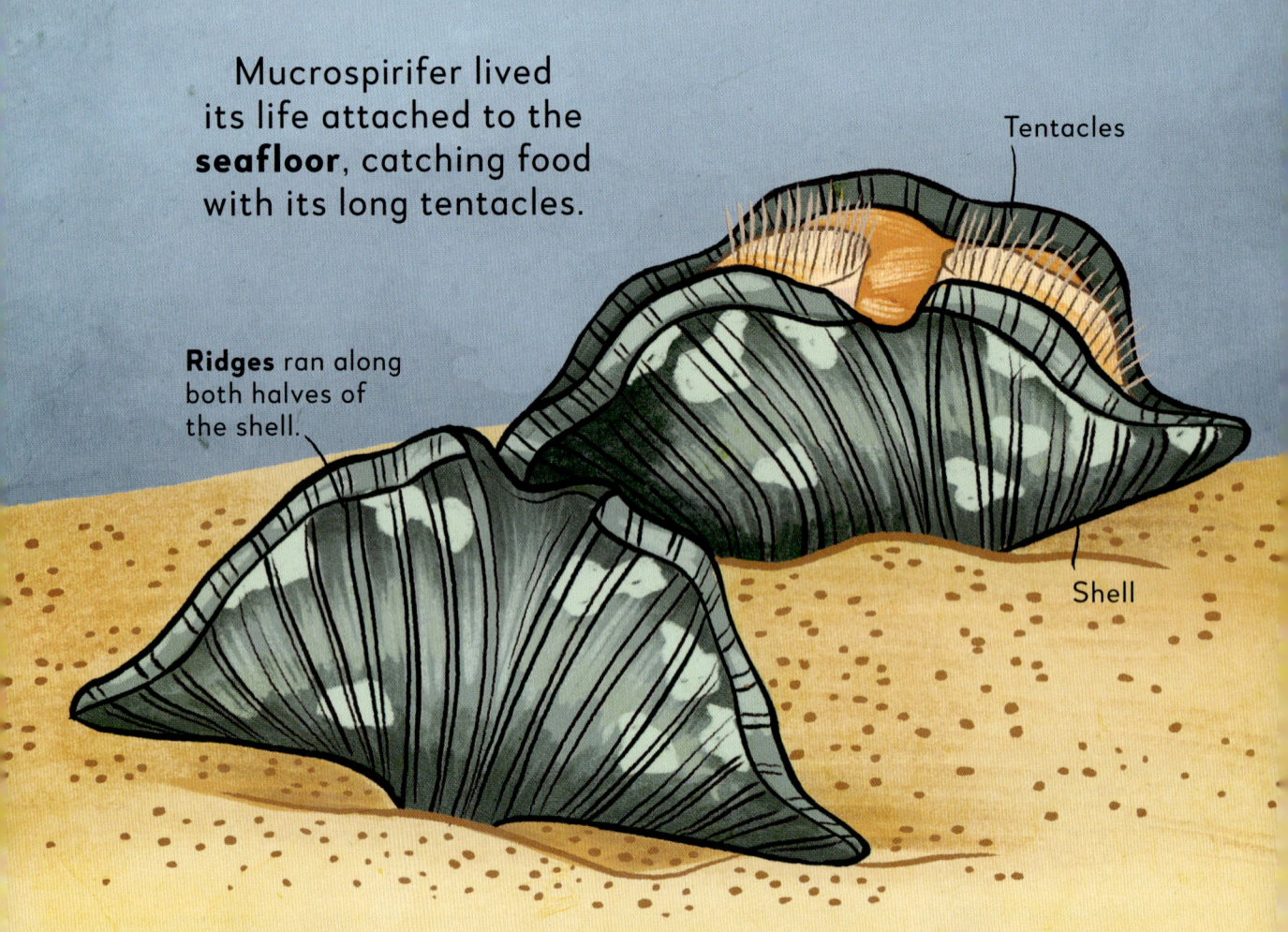

Mucrospirifer

(mew-kroh-SPIH-rih-fer)

Mucrospirifer was a type of sea creature called a **brachiopod**. These animals have a soft body protected by a hard shell. Mucrospirifer is nicknamed the **butterfly shell**.

Unlike spiders, Attercopus had a long **tail**.

Long body

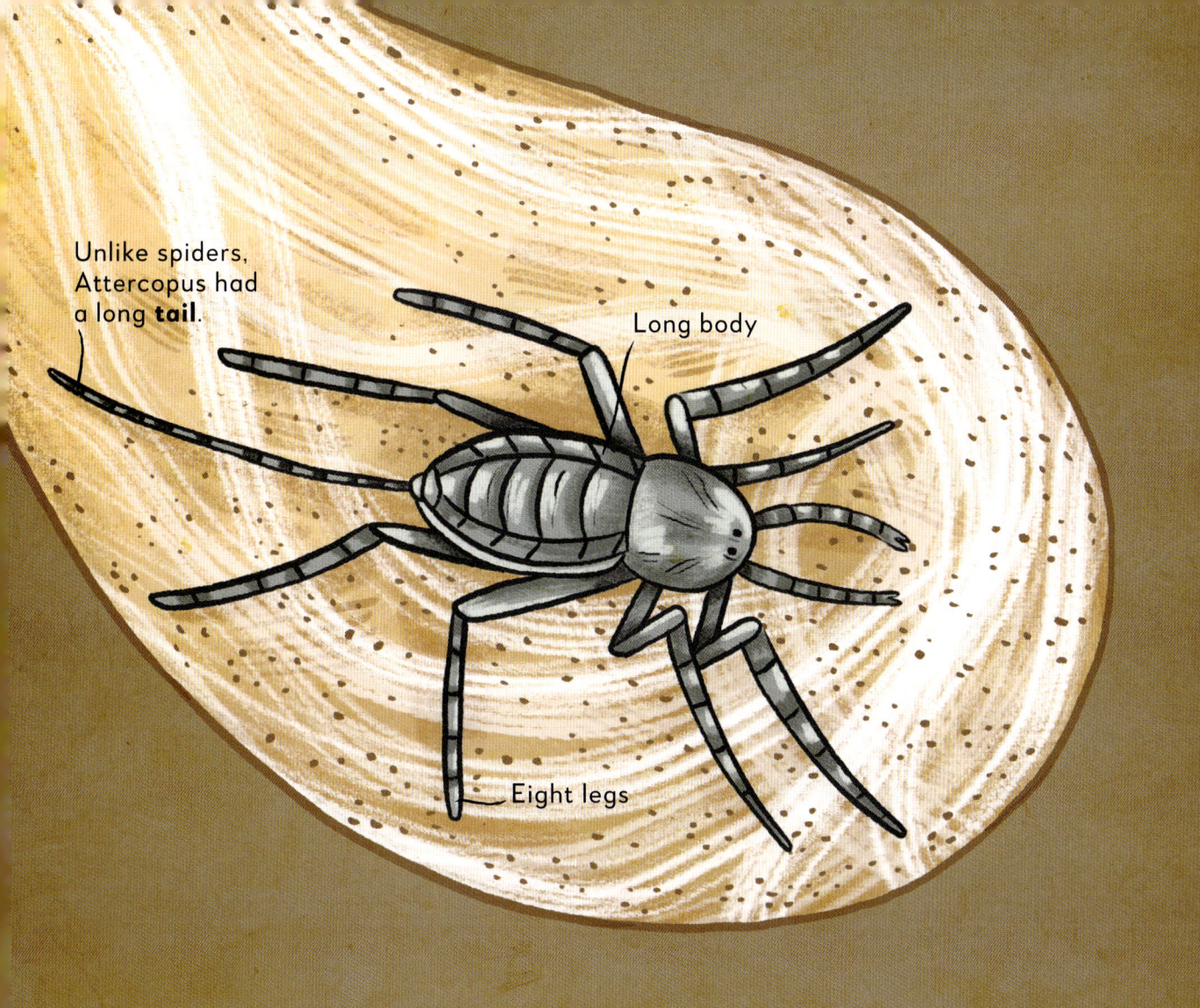

Eight legs

Attercopus

(a-ter-KOP-uss)

Attercopus was a close relative of **spiders** that lived 386 million years ago. It made threads of **stretchy** silk, but did not spin webs.

Devonian

Eusthenopteron

(yoos-theh-NOP-ter-on)

This fish had **strong** fins. It was related to the first animals with four legs, but it lived entirely in the **water** where it hunted smaller fish.

Scales

The strong **fins** were supported by bones.

Eusthenopteron could breathe underwater and in the air.

Instead of teeth, Dunkleosteus had bones shaped like blades in its jaws that could **slice** prey in half.

Powerful tail

Armoured head

Crunch!

Blade-like bones

Dunkleosteus

(dun-kel-OSS-tee-uss)

A **super** predator with one of the most powerful bites of any animal, Dunkleosteus was a **scary** fish. Armour covered its head, neck, and the front half of its body.

Devonian

Devonian swamp

For millions of years, large animals only lived in the **water**. It was in an ancient Devonian swamp where the first fish with fins like **legs** stepped onto land.

This fish had sharp teeth. It lived at the bottom of swamps and **surprised** its prey.

Laccognathus
(la-kog-NAY-thuss)

Archaeopteris
(ar-kee-OP-teh-riss)

Large **roots** helped to anchor this tree into the swampy ground.

Tiktaalik was one of the first fish to use its **leg-like** fins to drag itself out of the water.

Tiktaalik
(tik-TAH-lik)

Asterolepis was a fish that was covered in hard **armour**, including its paddle-like arms.

Asterolepis
(a-steh-ro-LEP-iss)

Fish with fins like legs were the ancestors of all four-legged animals.

Devonian

When swimming in rivers and lakes, Ichthyostega used its back legs to **steer**.

Fish-like tail

Strong arms

Unusually, Ichthyostega had **seven toes** on its back feet.

Ichthyostega
(ik-thee-oh-STEE-ga)

Ichthyostega was a type of early **amphibian**. It spent most of its time in water, but it could use its **strong** arms to pull itself onto land.

The flat top of the back fin was covered in small **spikes**.

Bumpy head

Whips

Long **whips** behind Stethacanthus' fins may have attracted mates.

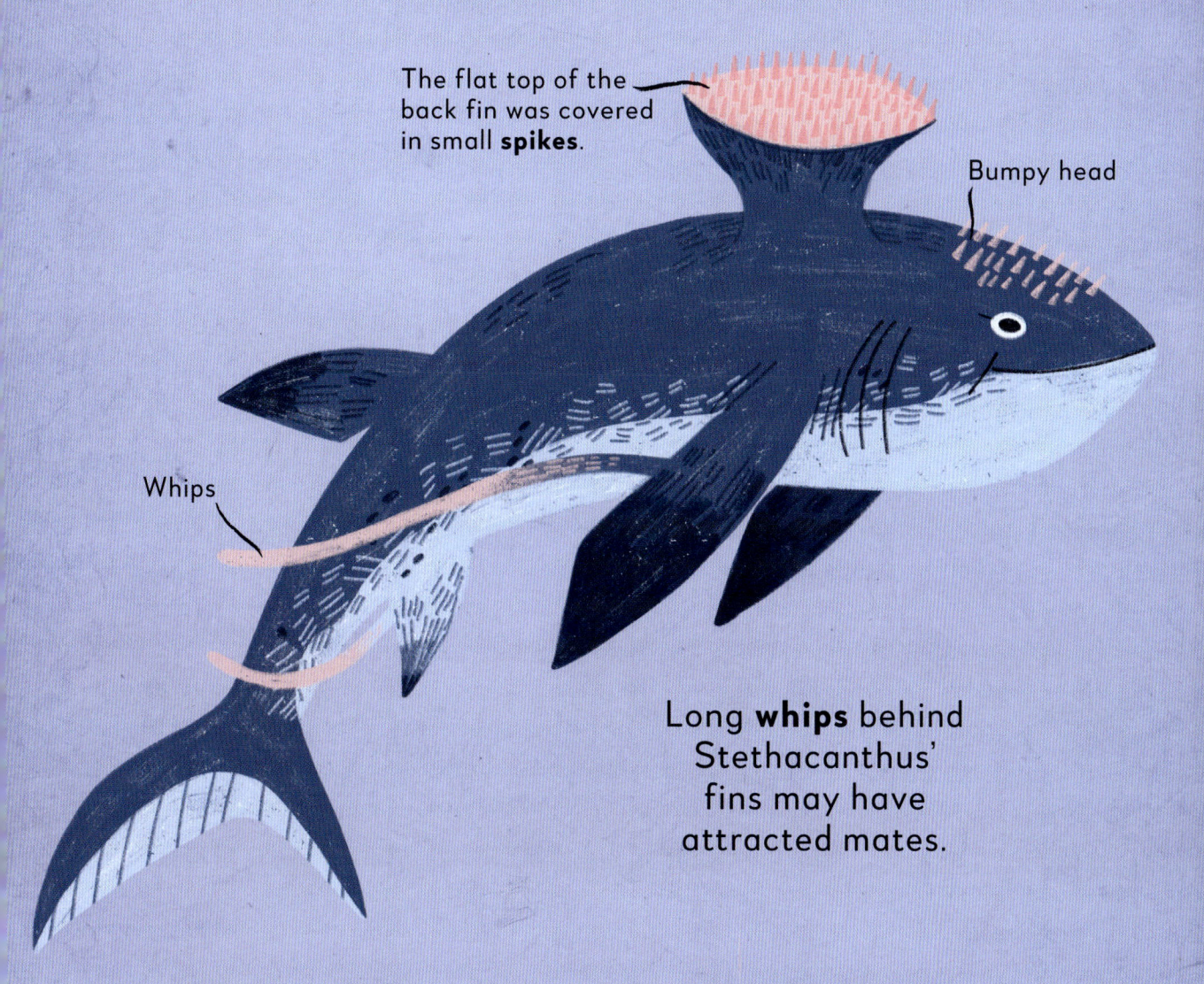

Stethacanthus

(steth-a-KAN-thuss)

This bizarre-looking fish was a distant cousin of **sharks**. Its back fin was shaped like an **ironing board**, and may have been used to show off to rivals.

Carboniferous

Calamites

(ka-la-MAI-teez)

Calamites was a type of plant called a horsetail. Large **forests** of them lived together in swampy areas. Each one could grow **taller** than a house.

The **branches** grew in rings around the trunk.

Straight trunk

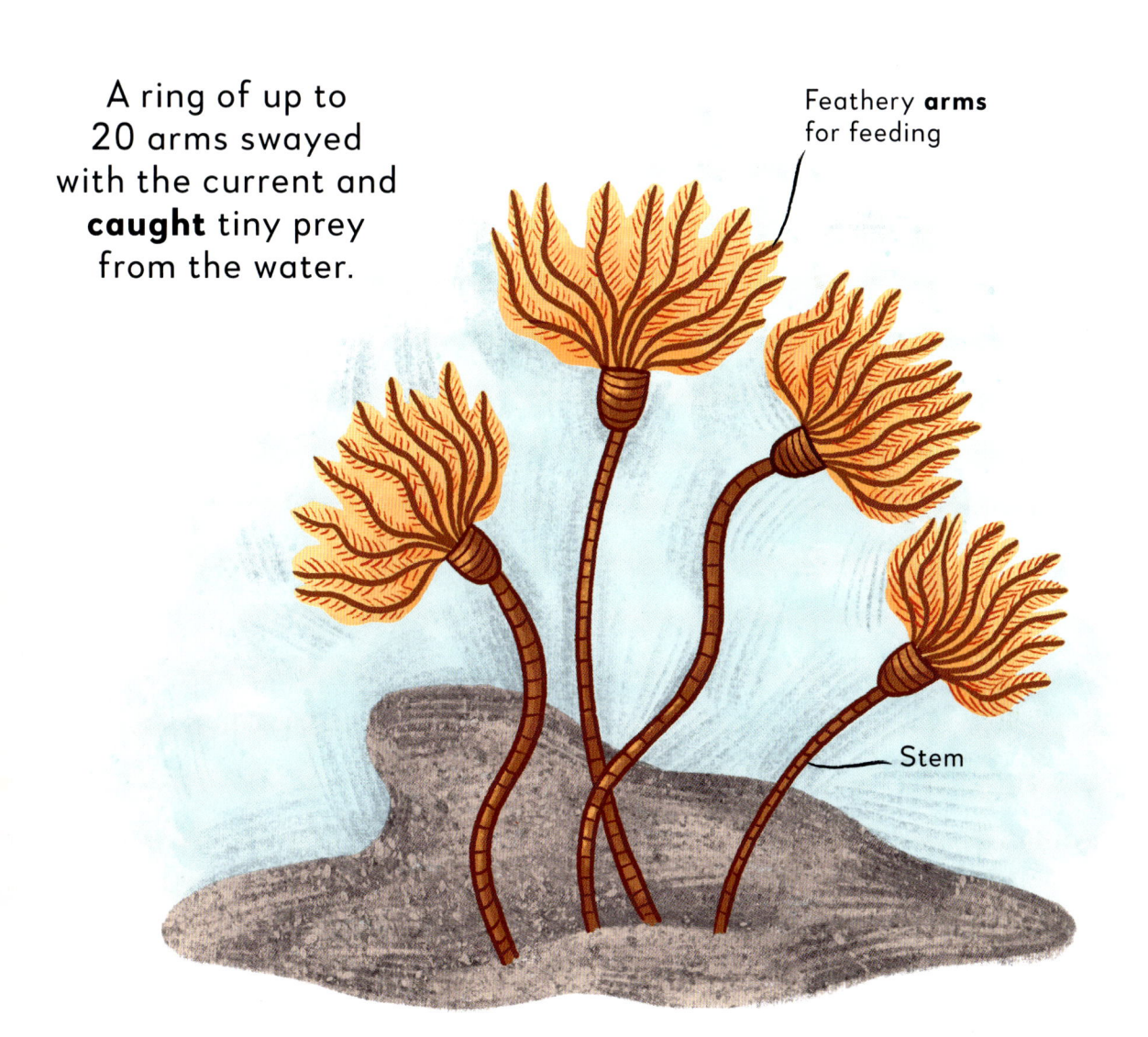

A ring of up to 20 arms swayed with the current and **caught** tiny prey from the water.

Feathery **arms** for feeding

Stem

Woodocrinus

(wud-oh-KRY-nuss)

Although it might look a bit like a **flower** on a long stem, Woodocrinus was a type of sea animal related to starfish, called a **crinoid**.

Carboniferous

Arthropleura
(arth-ro-PLOO-ra)

This supersized creepy-crawly was a type of giant **millipede** that was longer than most adult humans are tall. It lived in **swampy** forests and ate plants.

Arthropleura was the largest invertebrate to ever live on land.

Long body

Arthropleura may have had as many as 120 **legs**.

Feelers

Arthropleura was so big that it would only just have been able to fit through a **doorway**.

Carboniferous

Insects, like Meganeura, were the **first** animals to be able to **fly**.

Zoom!

Eyes

Wings

The spiny legs ended in claws that were used to **trap** prey.

Meganeura
(me-ga-NYOO-ra)

Around the size of a pigeon, Meganeura was the **largest** insect ever to have lived. It looked like a dragonfly and was a **speedy** predator that snatched its prey in mid-air.

Edaphosaurus
(eh-da-foh-SOR-uss)

This lizard-like plant eater was actually an early relative of furry mammals. It had a large **sail** that could absorb or release heat, to help warm up or cool down its body **temperature**.

Spines

The **spiky** sail was also used to scare away predators.

Tail

This was one of the largest land animals of its time.

Permian

Dimetrodon

(dai-MET-roh-don)

This meat eater was the first large land **predator**. It might look a bit like a dinosaur, but Dimetrodon lived millions of years **before** they appeared.

Dimetrodon was more closely related to mammals than to reptiles.

A large **sail** was used for showing off.

Sharp **teeth**

Long tail

40

Seymouria

(see-MOR-ee-a)

Seymouria was an early **amphibian**. About the size of a dog, this hunter had sharp, slender teeth to **snap** up insects and other small creatures.

Seymouria lived most of its life on **land** and only returned to water to lay its eggs.

Short neck

The **eggs** were laid in water like frogspawn.

Strong legs

Permian

Round body

Armour

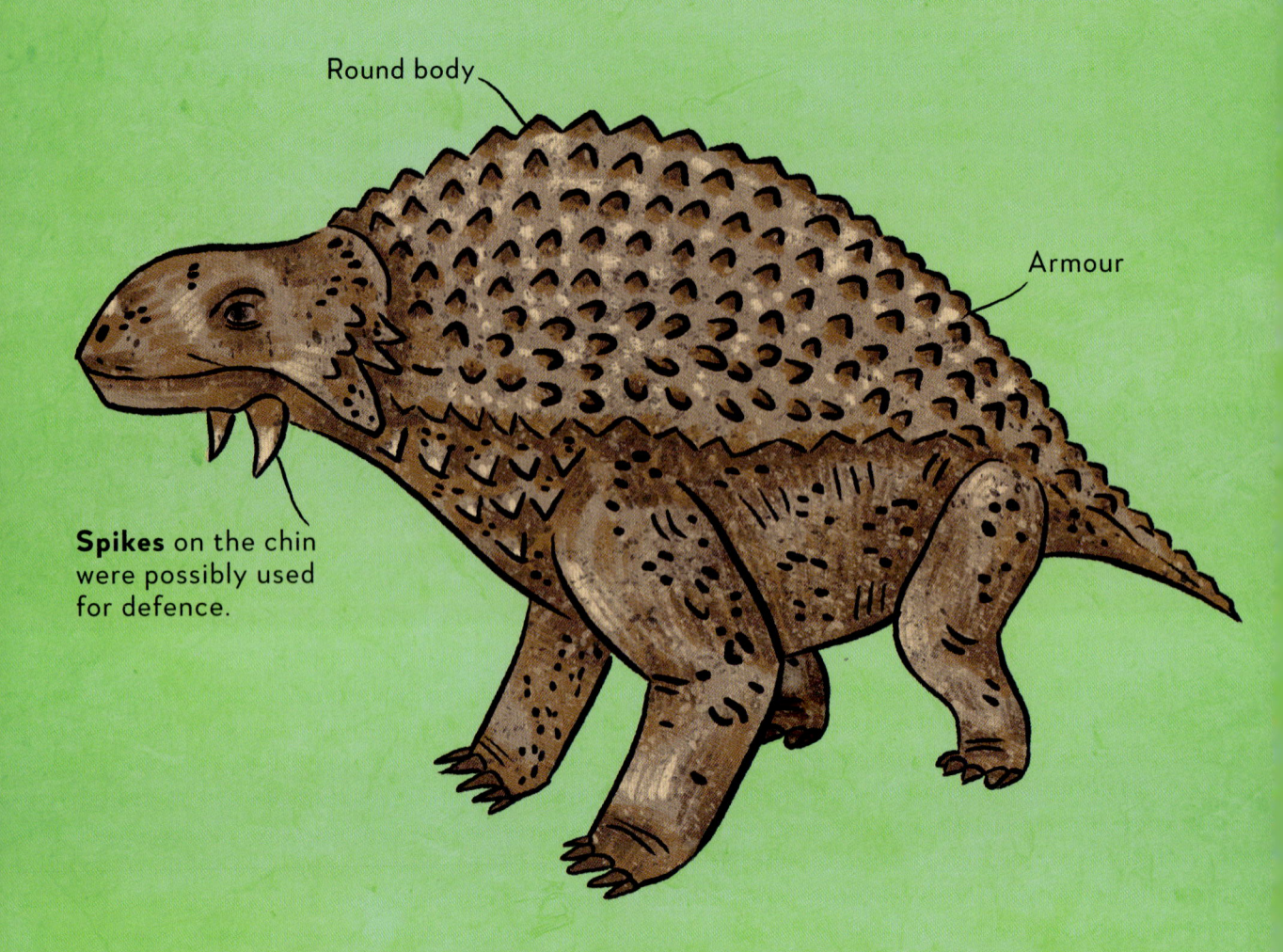

Spikes on the chin were possibly used for defence.

Scutosaurus

(skut-oh-SOR-uss)

This **chunky**, plant-eating reptile was as heavy as a cow. Its skin was **studded** with bony bumps that helped to protect it from predators.

Elginia

(el-GIN-ee-a)

Crawling low to the ground, Elginia hunted for plants to munch. This reptile is named after the town of Elgin in Scotland because that is where its **fossils** were discovered.

Large **horns** made Elginia look scarier to predators.

Scales

Short legs

Mesozoic Era

(mez-oh-ZOH-ik EE-ra)

Triassic Period
252–201 million years ago

The name Mesozoic means "middle life".

Jurassic Period
201–145 million years ago

◀ Paleozoic Era

The Mesozoic Era lasted from 252–66 million years ago. It was divided up into three **periods**. In this era, **reptiles** ruled the land, sky, and ocean.

Cretaceous Period
145–66 million years ago

Cenozoic Era ▶

Triassic

Nothosaurus

(noh-thoh-SOR-uss)

This sea reptile **hunted** its prey in shallow seas, but clambered onto land to rest and sleep. Using its sharp teeth, it **snapped up** fast-moving fish.

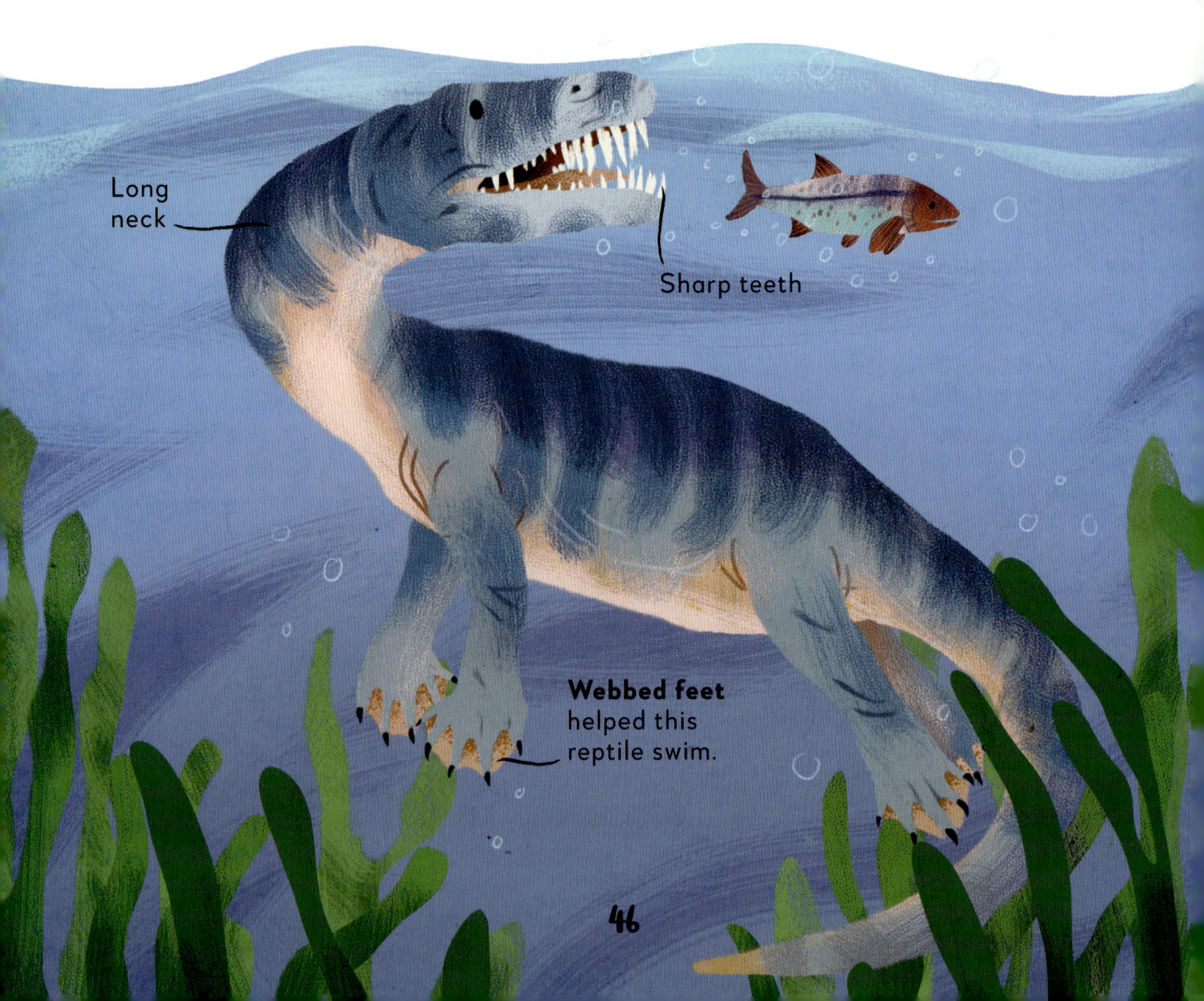

Long neck

Sharp teeth

Webbed feet helped this reptile swim.

Stagonolepis dug in the ground with its **snout**.

Armoured back

Similar to a **crocodile**, Stagonolepis was covered in rows of thick **armour plates** made of bone.

Stagonolepis

(stag-on-oh-LEP-iss)

This **reptile** lived towards the end of the Triassic Period. It was a plant eater that used its strong arms to **dig** for food.

Triassic

Triassic floodplain

Around 230 million years ago, there were **rivers** that often flooded the land around them. These areas were filled with animals, including the first **dinosaurs**.

Herrerasaurus
(heh-reh-ra-SOR-uss)

The **largest** meat-eating dinosaur of its time, Herrerasaurus had sharp claws and teeth.

Saurosuchus
(sor-oh-SOO-kuss)

Probably the top **predator** in its habitat, Saurosuchus was a reptile that hunted dinosaurs!

Fossils of all these animals can be found at a site called the "Valley of the Moon", in Argentina.

This little dinosaur was about as heavy as a pet **cat**.

Eodromaeus
(ee-oh-droh-MAY-uss)

This unusual reptile used its strong **beak** to dig up tough plants to eat.

Hyperodapedon
(hai-per-oh-dap-EE-don)

Triassic

Long snout

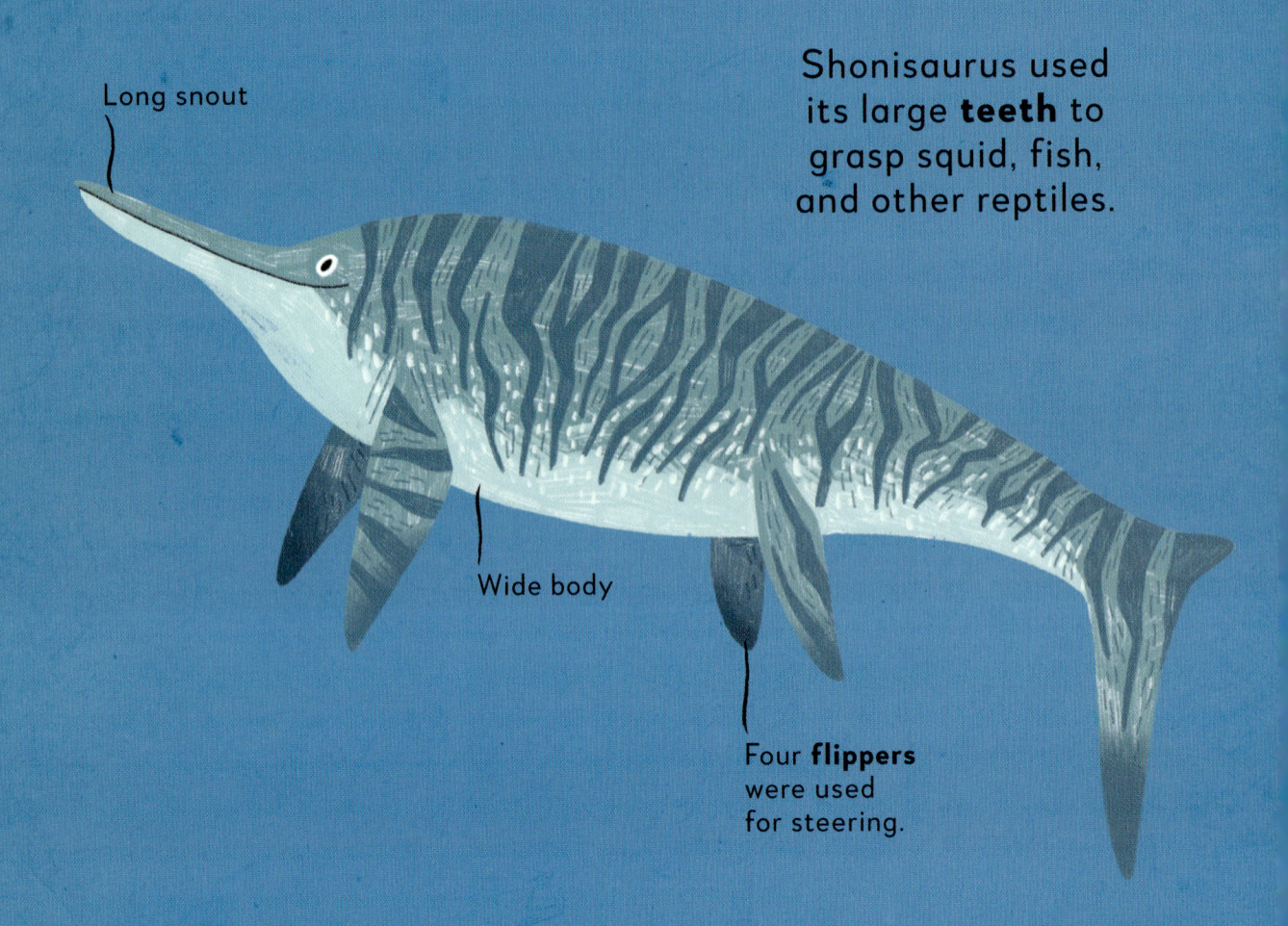

Shonisaurus used its large **teeth** to grasp squid, fish, and other reptiles.

Wide body

Four **flippers** were used for steering.

Shonisaurus

(sho-nee-SOR-uss)

Shonisaurus was one of the ichthyosaurs, which were sea reptiles with long snouts. It was also **enormous**, growing longer than a humpback **whale**.

Eoraptor

(ee-oh-RAP-tor)

Living around 230 million years ago in what is now Argentina, Eoraptor is one of the **earliest** known dinosaurs. It was only about the size of a **fox**.

Tail

Claws

Long legs

Triassic

Postosuchus was one of the top Triassic predators.

Huge head

Postosuchus walked on its back **legs**.

Coelophysis
(see-loh-FAI-siss)

This slender dinosaur was a **meat eater** that caught other small reptiles and fish. It was a speedy hunter that probably lived in **groups**.

Postosuchus

(post-oh-SOO-kuss)

This fearsome creature was an ancient relative of **crocodiles**. It lived alongside some of the first dinosaurs, which it **snacked** on.

A long **tail** was used for balance.

Coelophysis **fossils** are some of the most commonly found dinosaur remains from the Triassic Period.

Long neck

Narrow **jaws** were filled with sharp teeth.

Sharp **claws** were used for gripping small animals.

Jurassic

Ichthyosaurus
(ik-thee-oh-SOR-uss)

Ichthyosaurus might look like a dolphin or a fish, but this was a type of **sea reptile** called an **ichthyosaur**. It streaked through the water using its powerful tail.

Large **eyes** were good for spotting food in deep, dark water.

Pointed **teeth** were used to grab quick prey.

Fins were used for steering.

Ichthyosaurus was **discovered** more than 200 years ago. Many of its fossils have been found with their **last** meals of squid and fish inside their belly.

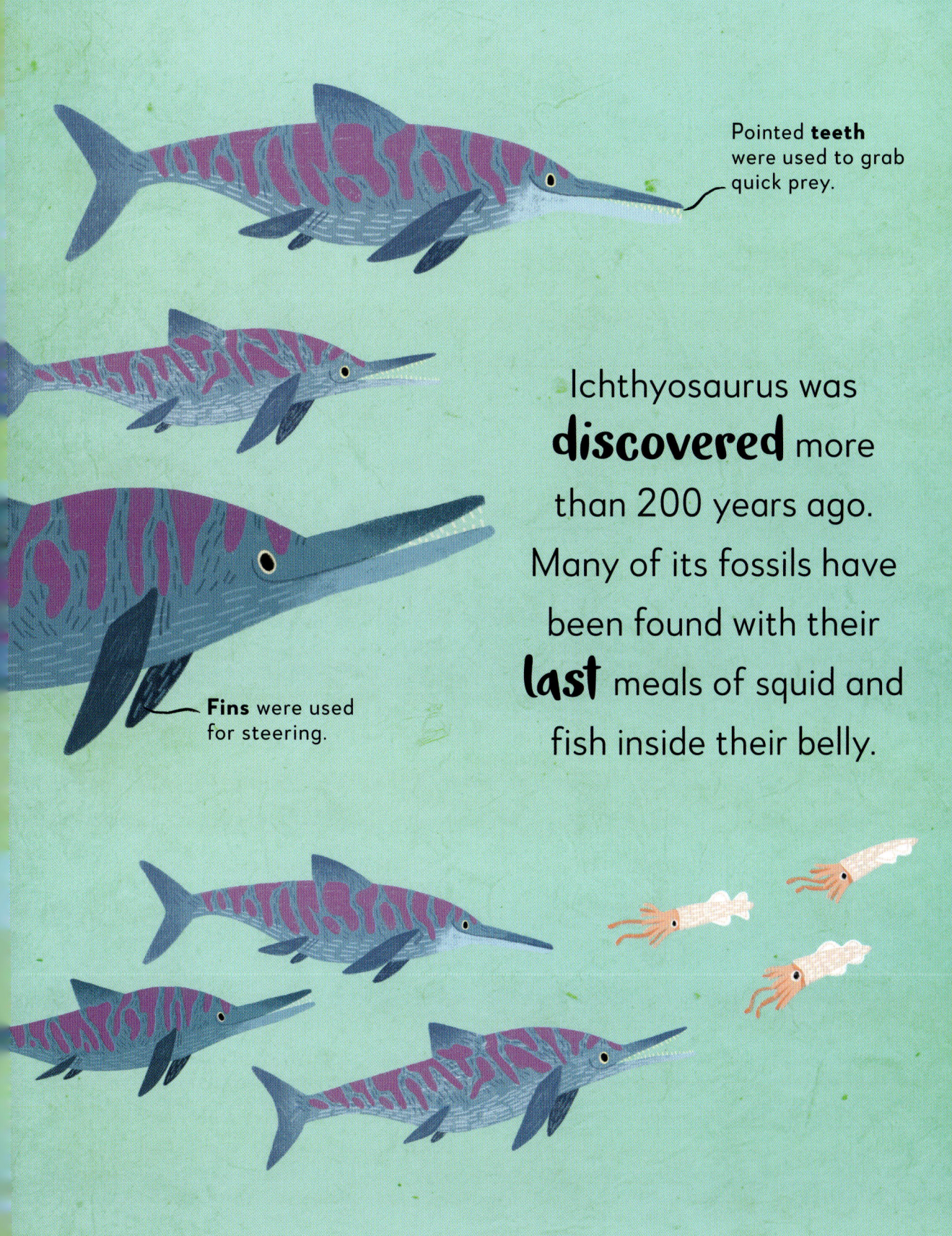

Jurassic

Dilophosaurus

(dai-loh-foh-SOR-uss)

This dinosaur was **named** Dilophosaurus, which means "two-crested lizard", because it had two tall head crests. They were probably used to **impress** mates.

The **crests** may have been brightly coloured.

Dilophosaurus was about twice as long as a **horse**.

Claws

Porcupine-like bristles ran along this dinosaur's back.

Tail

Bristles

Two pairs of **tusks** at the front of the dinosaur's mouth were used for defence and attack.

Heterodontosaurus

(het-eh-roh-don-toh-SOR-uss)

This **bristly** dinosaur was unusual because it had different types of **teeth** in its jaws. This shows that it ate both plants and animals.

Jurassic

Megazostrodon
(meh-ga-ZOSS-tro-don)

This little mammal **scurried** under the feet of dinosaurs. It avoided becoming their **dinner** by making its home inside burrows and in trees.

Megazostrodon probably slept in the day and came out at night.

Fur

Megazostrodon may have laid leathery-shelled **eggs**.

Sharp teeth

Crest

Cryolophosaurus probably had a few **feathers**.

A strange bony **crest** on this dinosaur's head helped it to attract mates.

Three sharp **claws** on each hand were used for slashing at prey.

Cryolophosaurus

(kry-oh-loh-foh-SOR-uss)

Cryolophosaurus was one of the largest and **deadliest** meat-eating dinosaurs of its day. Its fossils have been found in the continent of **Antarctica**.

Jurassic

Spiral shell

Gas inside an ammonite's shell helped it to float, and move up and down in the water – a bit like a **submarine**.

Grooves in shell

Arms

Dactylioceras

(dak-tai-lee-oh-SEH-rass)

Dactylioceras was an **ammonite**. Ammonites had a hard, spiral shell like a snail, but were similar to squid. They had around 10 wiggly **arms** to catch food.

Lepidotes

(leh-pi-DOH-tays)

Lepidotes was a common fish in Jurassic and Cretaceous seas and lakes. It **crushed** the shells of small sea creatures with hard, round **teeth**.

Round teeth

Tough scales

Tailfin

Lepidotes sometimes ended up as supper for hungry sea reptiles.

Jurassic

Liopleurodon
(lai-oh-PLYOO-roh-don)

This **scary** underwater predator was a type of huge sea reptile. Its short neck and big jaws gave it a **powerful** bite.

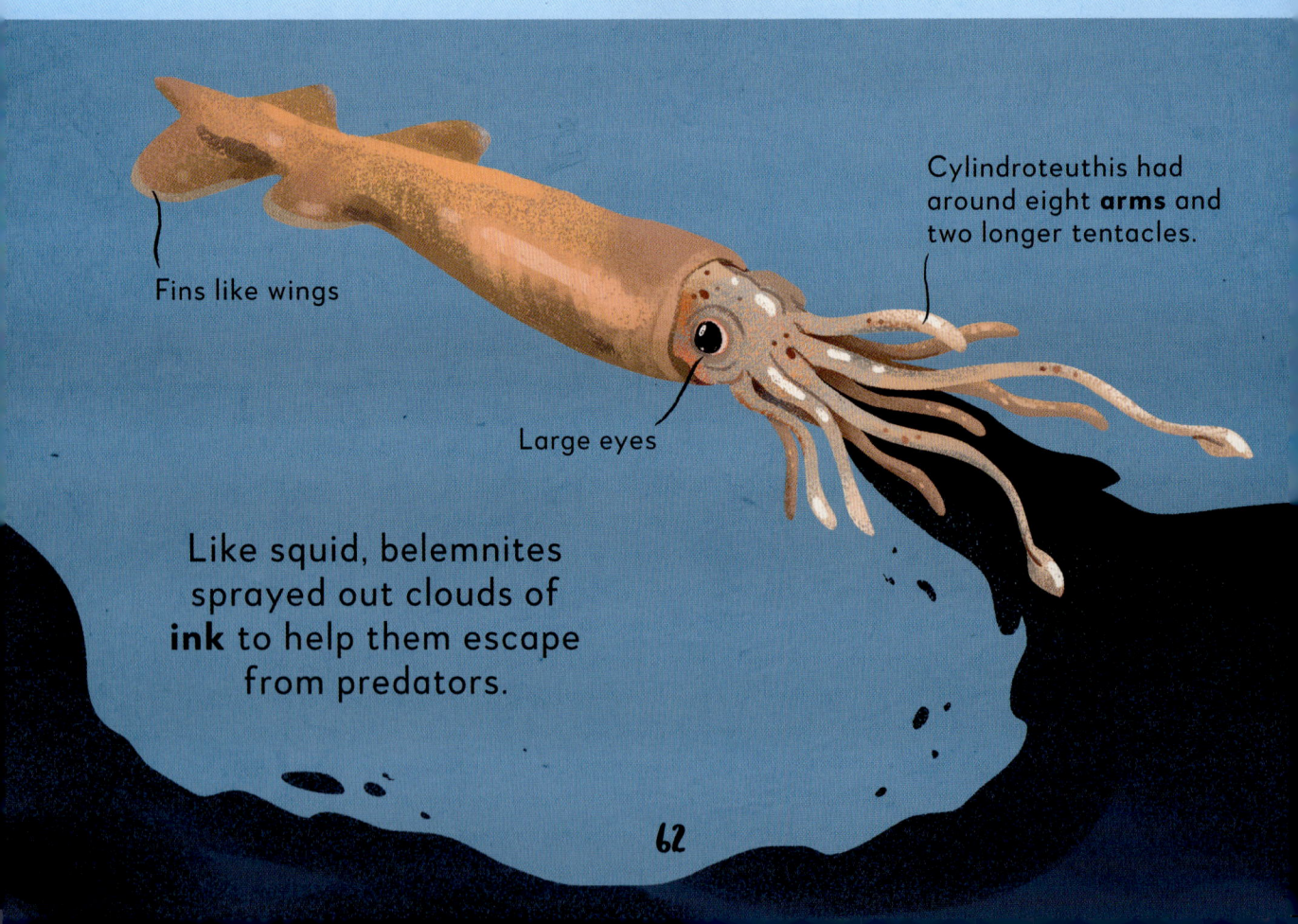

Cylindroteuthis had around eight **arms** and two longer tentacles.

Fins like wings

Large eyes

Like squid, belemnites sprayed out clouds of **ink** to help them escape from predators.

Nostrils

Pointed teeth

As a reptile, Liopleurodon still had to swim to the surface to **breathe**.

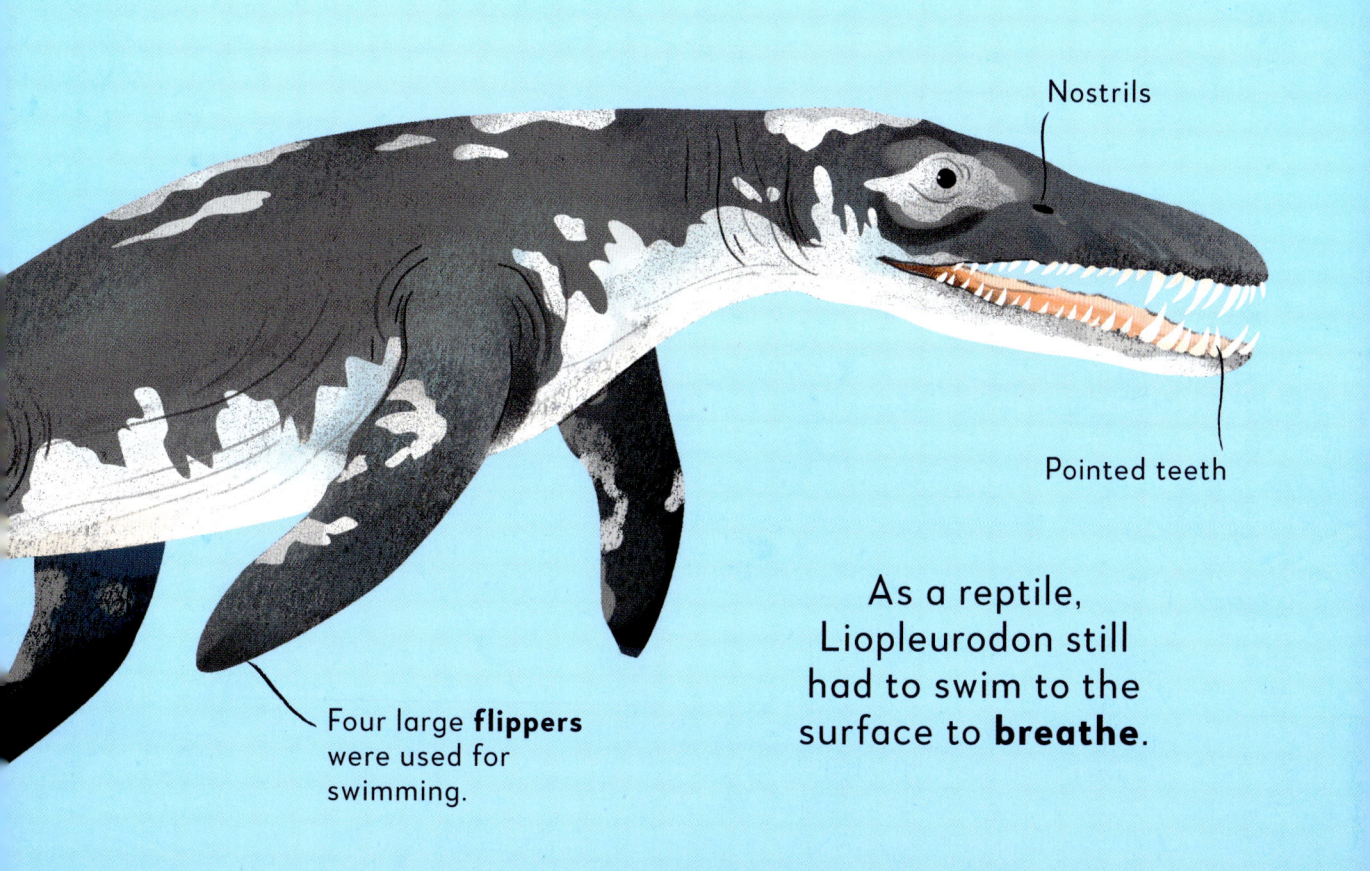

Four large **flippers** were used for swimming.

Cylindroteuthis

(si-lin-dro-TOO-thiss)

This animal was a **belemnite**, a type of creature that looked like a squid. It fed on fish, which have even been found **tangled** in its fossilized tentacles.

Jurassic

Yi had fuzzy **feathers** around its head, body, and arms.

Beak with teeth

Yi may have been able to glide from tree to tree using its **wings**.

Tail feathers

Yi

(YEE)

This might look a bit like a bat, but Yi was a dinosaur with **leathery** wings! It has the **shortest** name of any dinosaur.

Mamenchisaurus

(ma-men-chee-SOR-uss)

Mamenchisaurus was a whopping dinosaur that **weighed** as much as six elephants. It had one of the **longest** necks of any animal ever.

Small head

Mamenchisaurus was a plant-munching machine. It needed to **eat** a lot to keep up its energy.

A long **neck** helped this dinosaur to reach leaves at the tops of tall trees.

Long tail

Jurassic

The dinosaur's incredibly long tail could be used as a **weapon** to whip away hungry meat eaters.

Diplodocus was longer than two school buses!

Long tail

Spikes

Stegosaurus

(steg-oh-SOR-uss)

Although it ate plants, Stegosaurus could be a scary dinosaur. It was as big as an elephant, had large **plates** on its back, and sharp **spikes** on its tail.

Small head

Long neck

Diplodocus
(dip-LOD-oh-kuss)

This giant was one of the **longest** dinosaurs of all. It chomped on plants, and had teeth like **pegs** that it used to strip leaves from trees.

The tall **plates** were probably brightly coloured.

Four spikes on Stegosaurus' tail could be swung from side to side to keep **predators** away.

Neck shield

Jurassic

Jurassic islands

During the Jurassic Period, there were many small **islands** in some areas. These were home to all sorts of animals, as was the warm, **shallow** sea surrounding them.

Pterodactylus was a flying reptile, called a **pterosaur**. It swooped down on fish from the air.

Pterodactylus
(teh-roh-DAK-ti-luss)

Some lakes on the islands contained poisonous water.

This was a type of horseshoe crab. Some Mesolimulus fossils have been found next to their **footprints**.

Mesolimulus
(mez-oh-LIM-yoo-luss)

The pterosaur Rhamphorhynchus had a long tail with a small sail on the end, called a **vane**.

Rhamphorhynchus
(ram-fo-RINK-uss)

This was one of the first dinosaurs that looked like a **bird**. It had feathers and wings, but also teeth.

Archaeopteryx
(ar-kee-OP-teh-riks)

Compsognathus was a little **dinosaur** that hunted small creatures, such as lizards.

Compsognathus
(komp-sog-NAY-thuss)

Jurassic

Brachiosaurus

(brak-ee-oh-SOR-uss)

Twice the height of a giraffe, this *gigantic* plant eater was one of the tallest dinosaurs of all time. It could pluck leaves from some of the **highest** trees.

An adult Brachiosaurus weighed as much as **six** elephants! It needed strong, straight legs to support its huge body.

This dinosaur's neck was around 9 m (30 ft) long.

Cretaceous

Wuerhosaurus
(woo-eh-roh-SOR-uss)

About twice as heavy as a **rhino**, this dinosaur was a cousin of the more famous Stegosaurus. It **swung** its spiky tail at meat eaters that tried to attack it.

No one knows what shape Wuerhosaurus' plates were.

Plates ran along this dinosaur's neck, back, and tail.

Tail spikes

Beak

Spines

Some ammonites were the **size** of pennies, whereas others were as large as tractor tyres.

Arms

Many ammonites had curled spiral **shells**, but some had straight shells.

Crioceratites

(kree-oh-seh-ra-TAI-teez)

This curiously coiled creature looked like a squid with a shell, but it was an **ammonite**. Living in dangerous seas, its thin spines were its main **defence** against being eaten.

Cretaceous

Polacanthus
(pol-a-KAN-thuss)

Studded with sharp spikes and hard plates, Polacanthus was one of the best-defended dinosaurs. Its **vulnerable** belly was held close to the ground.

Large spikes

The **hips** were covered by a shield of bony armour for protection.

A **beak** lined with teeth was used for nibbling on plants.

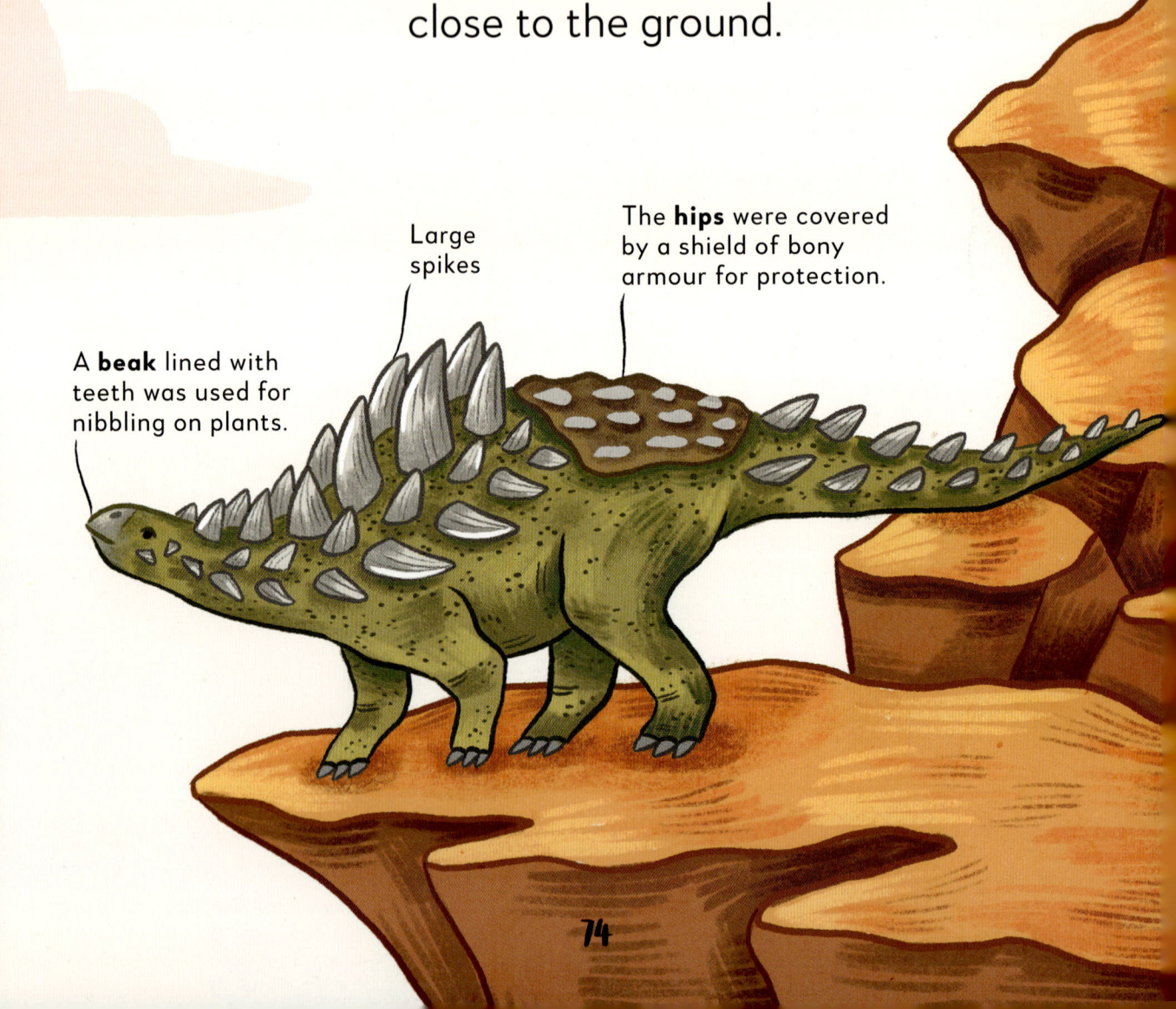

Iguanodon

(ig-WAH-noh-don)

This bulky plant eater lived in large **herds**. It had a sharp thumb spike on each hand that it used to gather plants and **scare off** predators.

Beak

Iguanodon could **walk** on two or four legs.

Cretaceous

The **snout** was long like a crocodile's.

Curved claws

Baryonyx

(ba-ree-ON-iks)

Baryonyx was one of the **biggest** meat eaters of its time. Its main weapon was a **killer claw** on each thumb. It ate fish and sometimes other dinosaurs.

Mei

(MAY)

A cousin of Velociraptor, chicken-sized Mei also had a curved killer claw on each foot. Its full **name**, Mei long, means "soundly sleeping **dragon**".

Feathery tail

Wings

Killer claw

Some fossils of Mei have been found in a **sleeping** position.

Cretaceous

Cretaceous forest

Around 125 million years ago, Cretaceous forests were filled with **life**. Little feathered dinosaurs hunted for insects and some of the **first** larger mammals appeared.

Badger-sized Repenomamus was the largest **mammal** that lived with dinosaurs.

Repenomamus
(rep-en-oh-MA-muss)

This dinosaur was red and white and it had a **stripy** tail.

Sinosauropteryx
(sai-noh-sor-OP-teh-riks)

This small bird flew around ancient forests. Males had a long **tail**, but females did not.

Confuciusornis
(kon-FYOO-shuss-or-niss)

Teenage Psittacosaurus would **babysit** younger members of their family.

Psittacosaurus
(si-ta-koh-SOR-uss)

79

Cretaceous

Pterodaustro
(teh-ruh-DOR-stroh)

Pterodaustro was not a dinosaur or a bird, but a flying reptile called a **pterosaur**. Pterosaurs were the first animals apart from insects to learn how to **fly**.

Pterodaustro spent most of its time along the **shores** of lakes and rivers.

Webbed feet

Large wings

Using its **bristly** beak Pterodaustro scooped up water and **filtered** out tiny animals between its long teeth, a bit like a flamingo.

The beak contained around 1,000 long **teeth** like needles.

Cretaceous

Changmiania
(chang-mee-a-NEE-a)

This little plant-eating dinosaur was about the size of a **chicken**. It was a fast runner and could quickly dash to its burrow to **escape** from danger.

This dinosaur was discovered curled up asleep.

Changmiania dug snug underground **burrows**.

Shovel-shaped snout

Big flower

U-shaped leaf

Archaeanthus was a tasty **snack** for plant-eating dinosaurs.

Archaeanthus

(ar-kee-AN-thuss)

This was one of the first **flowering** plants. It is a relative of the modern-day tulip tree and its blooms may have been **brightly** coloured.

Cretaceous

Nose sac

Tough beak

Muttaburrasaurus was named after the **town** of Muttaburra in Australia, where it was found.

Strong legs

Stomp!

Muttaburrasaurus
(muh-ta-buh-ra-SOR-uss)

This **chunky** dinosaur was a plant eater. It may have had a sac on its nose that could **inflate** like a balloon and make its calls louder.

Argentinosaurus
(ar-jen-tee-no-SOR-uss)

Heavier than twelve elephants and longer than three buses, this was one **huge** dinosaur. Enormous dinosaurs like this were called **titanosaurs**.

A very long **neck** was used to reach leaves from tall trees.

Stout legs

The front **feet** did not have any claws.

Argentinosaurus was one of the largest animals to ever walk on land!

Cretaceous

A tall sail on Spinosaurus' back made it look even scarier.

Sail

A crocodile-like **snout** contained lots of sharp teeth.

Three large claws

Spinosaurus

(spy-noh-SOR-uss)

Spinosaurus is the **biggest** meat-eating dinosaur ever discovered. Unusually, it could swim using its flat tail like a paddle, and it hunted fish that were as big as **cars**.

Deinosuchus

(dai-noh-SOO-kuss)

Four times longer than a horse, this **giant** cousin of the crocodile was a deadly predator. It waited patiently, then **lunged** out of the water at its prey.

Deinosuchus had a bone-crunching **bite** more powerful than that of any animal alive today.

Teeth

Tough skin

Splash!

Cretaceous

Maiasaura
(mai-a-SOR-a)

Maiasaura was a plodding plant eater that **nested** in big groups. These dinosaurs laid their eggs around the same time so that all their **babies** were born together.

Newly hatched Maiasaura could not walk and stayed in the **nest** for safety.

Maiasaura means "good mother lizard".

Adult

Maiasaura parents brought **food** to their young and guarded them.

Cretaceous

Euoplocephalus
(yoo-oh-ploh-KEF-a-luss)

This armoured dinosaur was built like a **tank**. Its thick skin had rows of bony bumps and **spikes** that helped to protect it from predators on the hunt for lunch.

Spikes

Wide body

Tail club

The huge tail club could be swung at enemies.

Lambeosaurus

(lam-bee-oh-SOR-uss)

This **hefty** plant eater was as large as an elephant. It had a head crest that was hollow and may have allowed this dinosaur to make **loud noises**.

The **head crest** was probably brightly coloured.

Duck-like beak

Inside the beak were hundreds of teeth arranged in **rows** to slice plants.

Cretaceous

Feathers helped this dinosaur stay warm.

Sharp teeth

Velociraptor may have lived together in **packs**.

An extra large **killer claw** was used to stab prey.

Velociraptor
(veh-LOSS-ih-rap-tor)

Velociraptor was about the size of a **turkey**. This dinosaur could run fast to chase prey, including other small dinosaurs. It had fluffy **feathers**, but it could not fly.

Archelon

(AR-keh-lon)

With a shell about the size of a small car, this huge **turtle** was the largest of all time. Its sharp beak was perfect for **snapping** up squid and jellyfish.

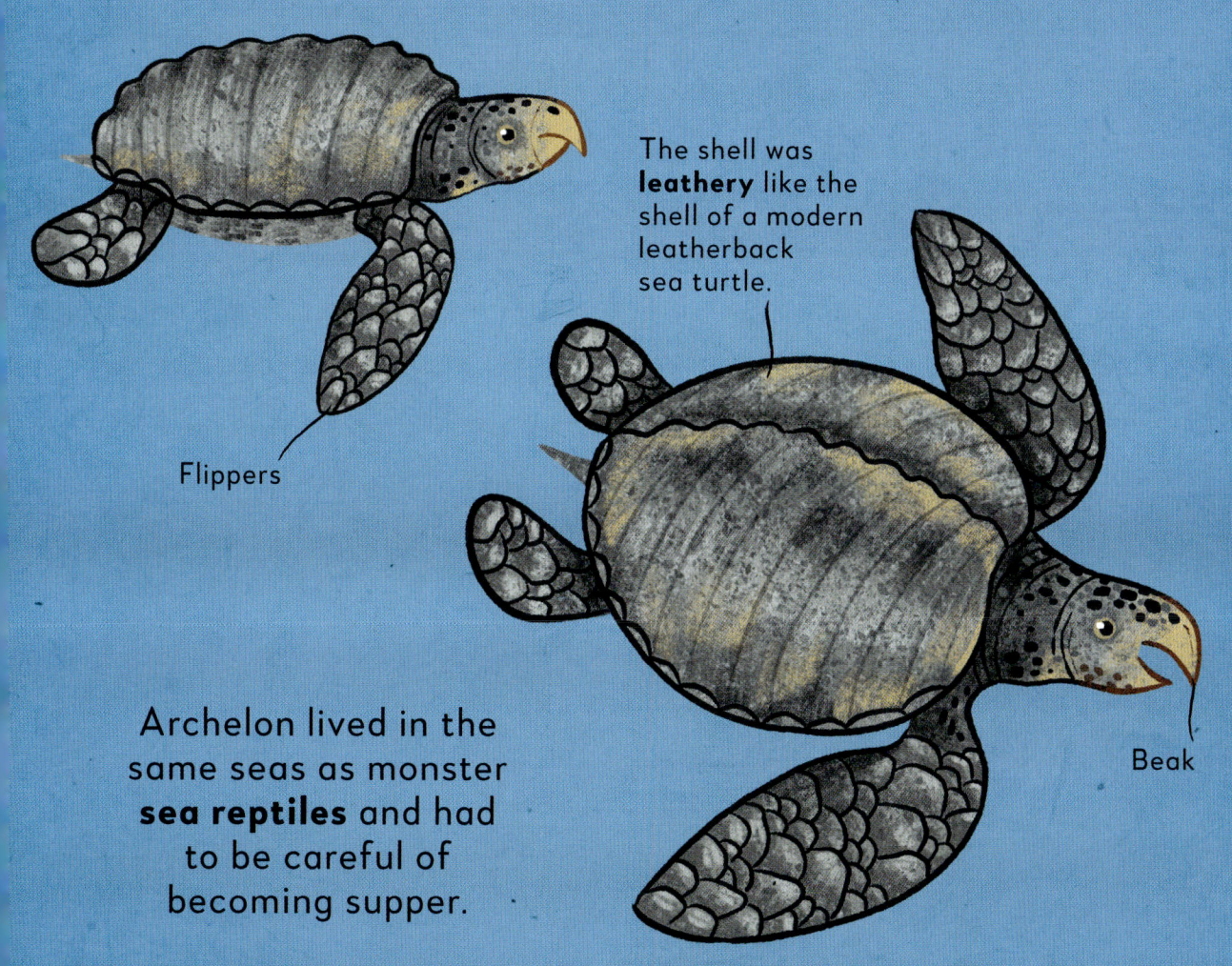

The shell was **leathery** like the shell of a modern leatherback sea turtle.

Flippers

Archelon lived in the same seas as monster **sea reptiles** and had to be careful of becoming supper.

Beak

Cretaceous

Eggs

Feathery wings were used to protect the **eggs** and keep them warm.

Feathers

Citipati

(sit-ee-PAH-tee)

Fossils of this dinosaur have been found **snuggled** in the centre of hill-shaped nests filled with eggs. Citipati looked after its eggs just like **birds** do today.

Albertonectes

(al-ber-toh-NEK-teez)

This sea reptile **paddled** in the ocean. Its neck was three times longer than a giraffe's and it snatched unsuspecting **fish** from their shoals.

Long neck

The four **flippers** were shaped like wings.

Small head

Cretaceous

Einiosaurus

(ai-nee-oh-SOR-uss)

Einiosaurus was a cousin of Triceratops and about the size of a rhino. **Bone beds** containing many fossils of this dinosaur suggest it lived in large **herds**.

Big **spikes** at the top of the frill were used for defence and display.

Large frill

Curved nose horn

Mosasaurus

(moh-za-SOR-uss)

This **gigantic** reptile lived in the sea. It had flat **flippers** that helped it to swim and steer as it chased down its prey.

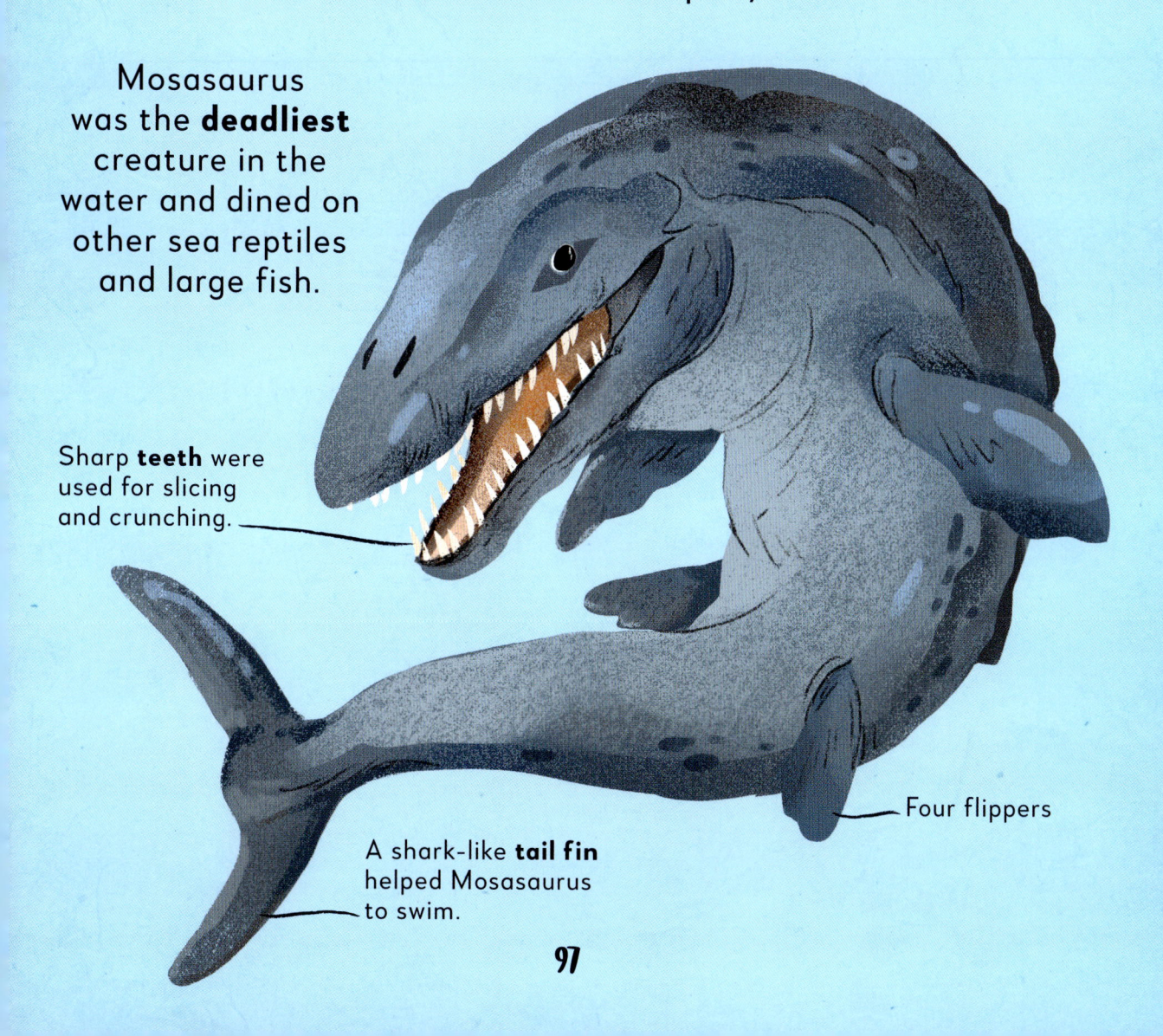

Mosasaurus was the **deadliest** creature in the water and dined on other sea reptiles and large fish.

Sharp **teeth** were used for slicing and crunching.

Four flippers

A shark-like **tail fin** helped Mosasaurus to swim.

Cretaceous

Feathered arms

Arms with feathery wings probably helped Gallimimus to **balance** when running at high speeds.

Beak

Long legs

Gallimimus

(ga-lee-MAI-muss)

These reptiles looked a bit like ostriches. They were among the **fastest** of all the dinosaurs, which helped them run away from **danger**.

Deinocheirus

(dai-no-KAI-russ)

This **odd-looking** dinosaur was related to meat eaters, but it ate only plants. Its large **claws** were used to pull down branches so it could pluck off the leaves.

The duck-like **beak** didn't have any teeth.

A **hump** on Deinocheirus' back made it look larger and may have scared away predators.

Long claws

Cretaceous

This is one of the largest meat-eating dinosaurs discovered in India.

Sharp teeth

Short arms

Strong legs

Indosuchus

(in-doh-SOO-kuss)

This **toothy** predator had very short arms for its size. Instead, Indosuchus did all its fighting and **biting** with its huge jaws.

Head crest

Beak

The large **wings** were kept folded when Quetzalcoatlus walked on land.

Whoosh!

Standing as tall as a **giraffe**, this pterosaur needed big meals. It even ate small dinosaurs.

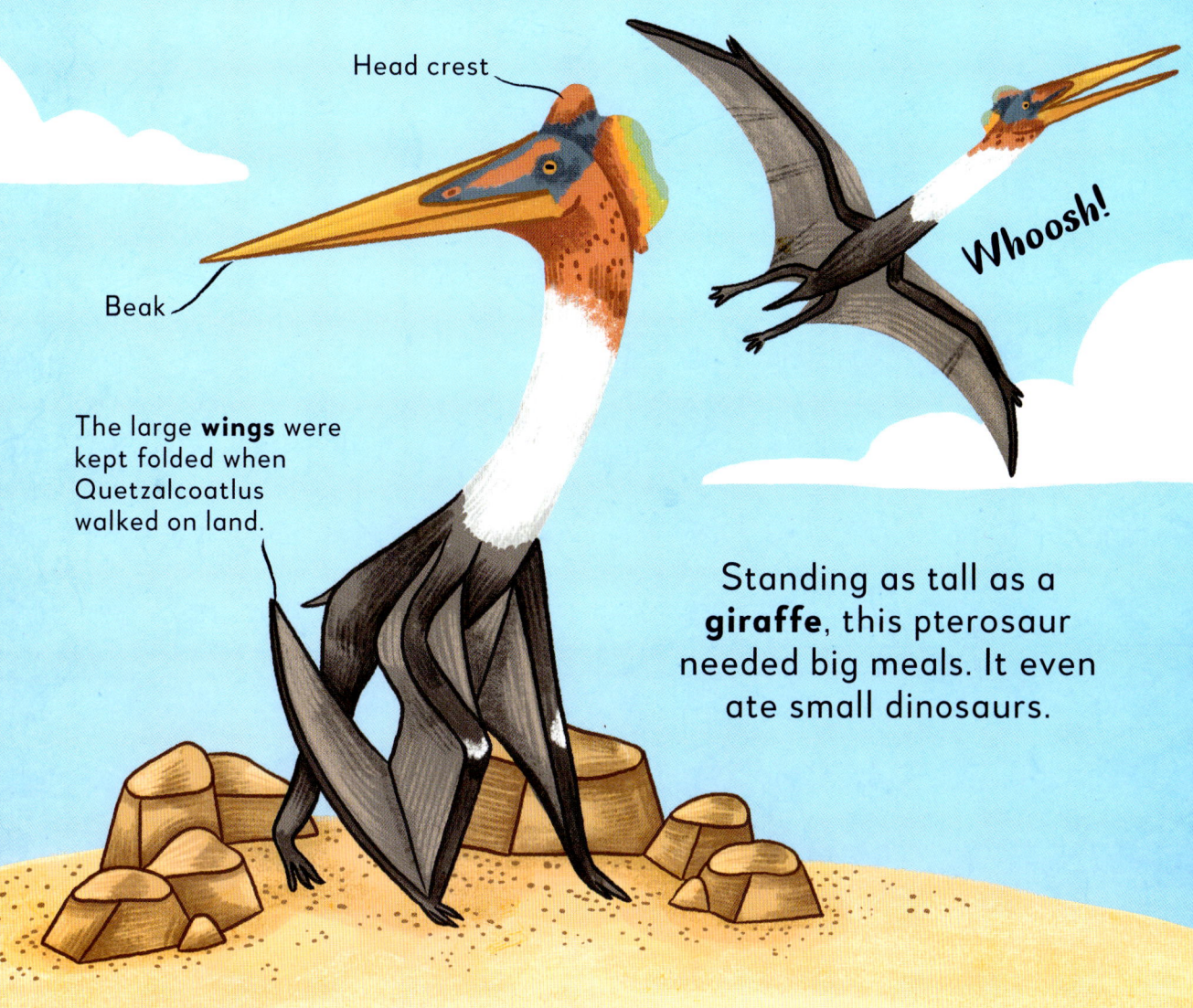

Quetzalcoatlus

(kwets-al-koh-AT-luss)

Quetzalcoatlus was a pterosaur, or flying reptile, with the wingspan of a small **aircraft**. It used its long beak to **snap** up prey, a bit like a stork.

Cretaceous

Pachycephalosaurus

(pak-ee-sef-a-lo-SOR-uss)

This bony-headed beast probably **head-butted** rivals to show which dinosaur was the strongest. It mostly ate plants but may have **eaten** some meat.

A thick, domed head was made of solid **bone**.

Nose spikes

Short arms

Pachycephalosaurus **means** "thick-headed lizard". Its bony head dome was thicker than a pencil is long.

An enormous **frill** with spikes protected Triceratops' neck.

Brow horns

Nose horn

Triceratops

(try-SEH-ra-tops)

As big and heavy as an elephant, this dinosaur was a **mega** plant eater. Triceratops had two long brow horns and a nose horn to help it **fight** its enemies.

Cretaceous

Roooooooooar!

The **jaws** had more than 50 teeth that could crunch bone.

Short **arms** ended in two curved claws.

Tyrannosaurus
(tai-ran-oh-SOR-uss)

Chomping its prey into pieces, Tyrannosaurus was the **deadliest** of all the meat-eating dinosaurs. This massive predator could even take on giant Triceratops.

Tyrannosaurus had the most **powerful** bite of any dinosaur!

Strong **legs** helped support Tyrannosaurus' huge weight.

Cenozoic Era

(seh-noh-ZOH-ik EE-ra)

The name Cenozoic means "new life."

Paleogene Period
66–23 million years ago

◂ Mesozoic Era

The Cenozoic Era began 66 million years ago and is the time that we are living in today. It is divided into three **periods**. **Mammals** have thrived in this era.

Neogene Period
23–2.6 million years ago

Quaternary Period
2.6 million years ago – present

Paleogene

Titanoboa

(tai-tan-oh-BOH-a)

This huge snake lived around 60 million years ago. It swam in **swamps** and ate large fish, turtles, and crocodiles, swallowing them in one huge **gulp**.

This enormous reptile was the largest snake to ever live.

Huge jaws

Long body

The sharp teeth **curved** backwards.

Wings

Big ears

Unlike modern bats, Icaronycteris had a long **tail**.

Just like bats today, Icaronycteris had a taste for insects, especially moths.

Icaronycteris

(ik-a-roh-nik-TEH-riss)

At around 52 million years old, this is the **earliest** known bat. It slept in the day, hanging upside down from branches, and hunted for food at **night**.

Paleogene

Ambulocetus is known as the "walking whale".

Webbed feet helped to push Ambulocetus through the water.

Fur

Long jaws

Ambulocetus
(am-byoo-loh-SEE-tuss)

This **mammal** might look a bit like a beaver or a platypus, but Ambulocetus was an early type of **whale**. It swam in the water and walked on land.

Banksia archaeocarpa

(BANK-see-a ar-kee-oh-KAR-pa)

This prehistoric plant is closely related to modern-day **wildflowers** that are found in Australia. The only fossils we have of it are of the **cones** that once contained its seeds.

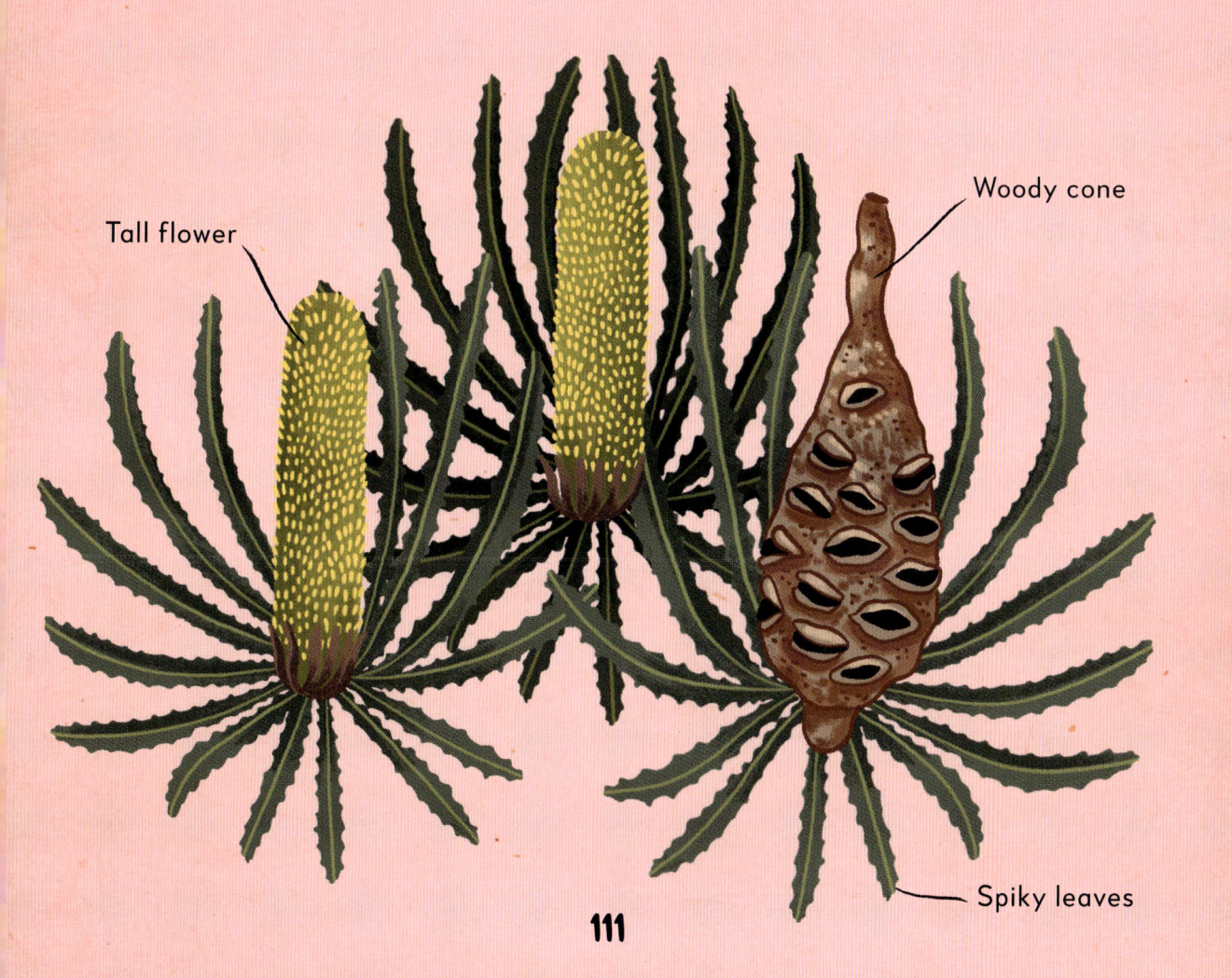

Tall flower

Woody cone

Spiky leaves

Paleogene

Long tail

Large eyes

Eosimias

(ee-oh-SIM-ee-uss)

This **mini** mammal was small enough to hold in your hand. Eosimias was an ancient cousin of monkeys and apes, and **jumped** through the trees.

Sharp teeth

Strong jaws

Andrewsarchus had **hooves** instead of claws.

Andrewsarchus
(an-droo-SAR-kuss)

This **toothy** beast was related to hippos and whales. With a skull twice as long as a bear's, it is thought to be the largest meat-eating mammal to have lived on **land**.

Paleogene

Basilosaurus

(ba-sil-oh-SOR-uss)

Basilosaurus was the first truly **gigantic** whale. It was almost twice as long as a bus and lived in the ocean, where it was a top predator that **hunted** other whales.

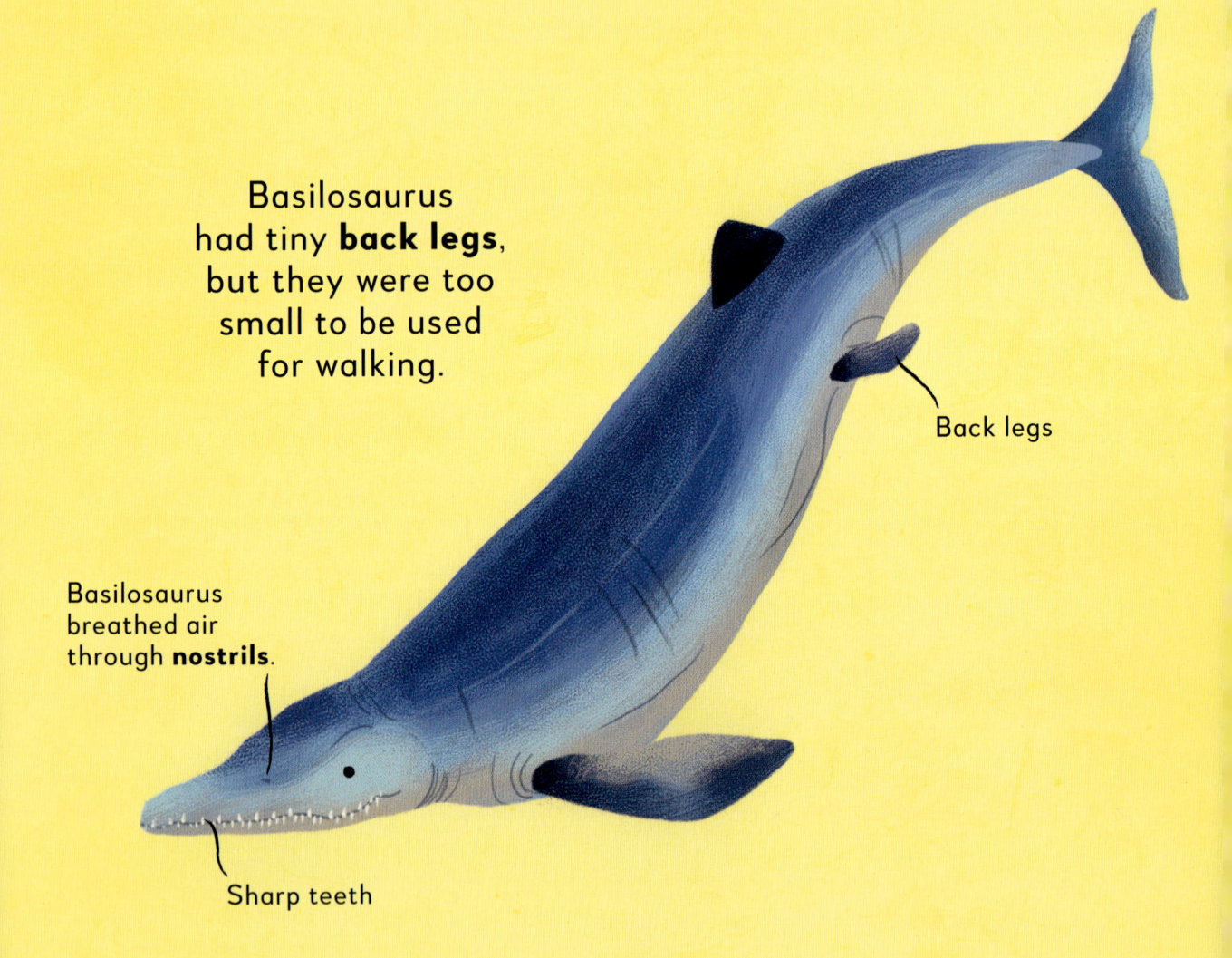

Basilosaurus had tiny **back legs**, but they were too small to be used for walking.

Back legs

Basilosaurus breathed air through **nostrils**.

Sharp teeth

Anthropornis

(an-throp-OR-niss)

Standing **taller** than many adult humans, this might have been the largest penguin ever. Like penguins today, it lived on land and hunted for food in the **sea**.

Waterproof feathers

Anthropornis had a pointed **beak** that was longer than a modern penguin's.

Webbed feet

Paleogene

Paleogene plains

Lots of animals called wide, grassy plains **home** during the Paleogene Period. With the disappearance of the large dinosaurs, mammals took over and **ruled** the world.

Rhino-like Uintatherium had large, knobbly **horns** on its head.

Uintatherium
(yoo-in-ta-THEER-ee-um)

Gastornis was a giant flightless **bird** with a big head. It probably ate fruit and seeds.

Gastornis
(gas-TOR-niss)

It was much warmer in the Paleogene Period than it is today.

Mesonyx was a **wolf-like** mammal with hooves. It might have hunted prey in packs.

Mesonyx
(mez-ON-iks)

This early horse had three **toes**. The middle toe was the largest.

Mesohippus
(mez-oh-HIP-uss)

Paleogene

Long neck

A bendy **upper lip** was used to grab leaves.

Paraceratherium was a type of gigantic **rhinoceros** without any horns. It lived around 30 million years ago.

Three toes

Paraceratherium
(pa-ra-seh-ra-THEER-ee-um)

Taller than a giraffe and weighing as much as three elephants, this was the **largest** mammal to ever live on land. It ate leaves from the **tops** of trees.

Palaeocastor

(pay-lee-oh-KASS-tor)

Palaeocastor was an ancient beaver that dug **spiral** burrows. At the bottom of each spiral was a **hollow** where the beaver family lived.

Fossils of the spiral burrows show that they could be 3 m (10 ft) **deep**.

Palaeocastor used its **sharp teeth** to gnaw into the ground.

Short tail

Neogene

Amphicyon wrestled its prey to the ground.

Powerful body

Amphicyon had pointed **teeth** for tearing meat.

Claws

Amphicyon

(am-fee-SAI-on)

Amphicyon looked like a **mix** between a dog and a bear. This meat-eating mammal was a top hunter with a powerful bite for **chomping** through bones.

Megalodon
(MEH-ga-loh-don)

This **mighty** shark was three times longer than the largest great white shark! It had a **superstrong** bite for gobbling up whales and other fish.

Powerful tail

Huge teeth

Neogene

Long snout

The curved **claws** were used to gather plants and battle predators.

Large claws

Three **toes** on each foot

Chalicotherium

(ka-li-koh-THEER-ee-um)

This **odd-looking** mammal was related to rhinoceroses and horses. Its arms were longer than its legs and it probably walked on its **knuckles**.

Platybelodon

(plat-ee-BEL-oh-don)

Platybelodon was an elephant-like animal known as a **shovel-tusker**. Using its flat lower tusks, it stripped bark from trees and sliced through **tough** plants.

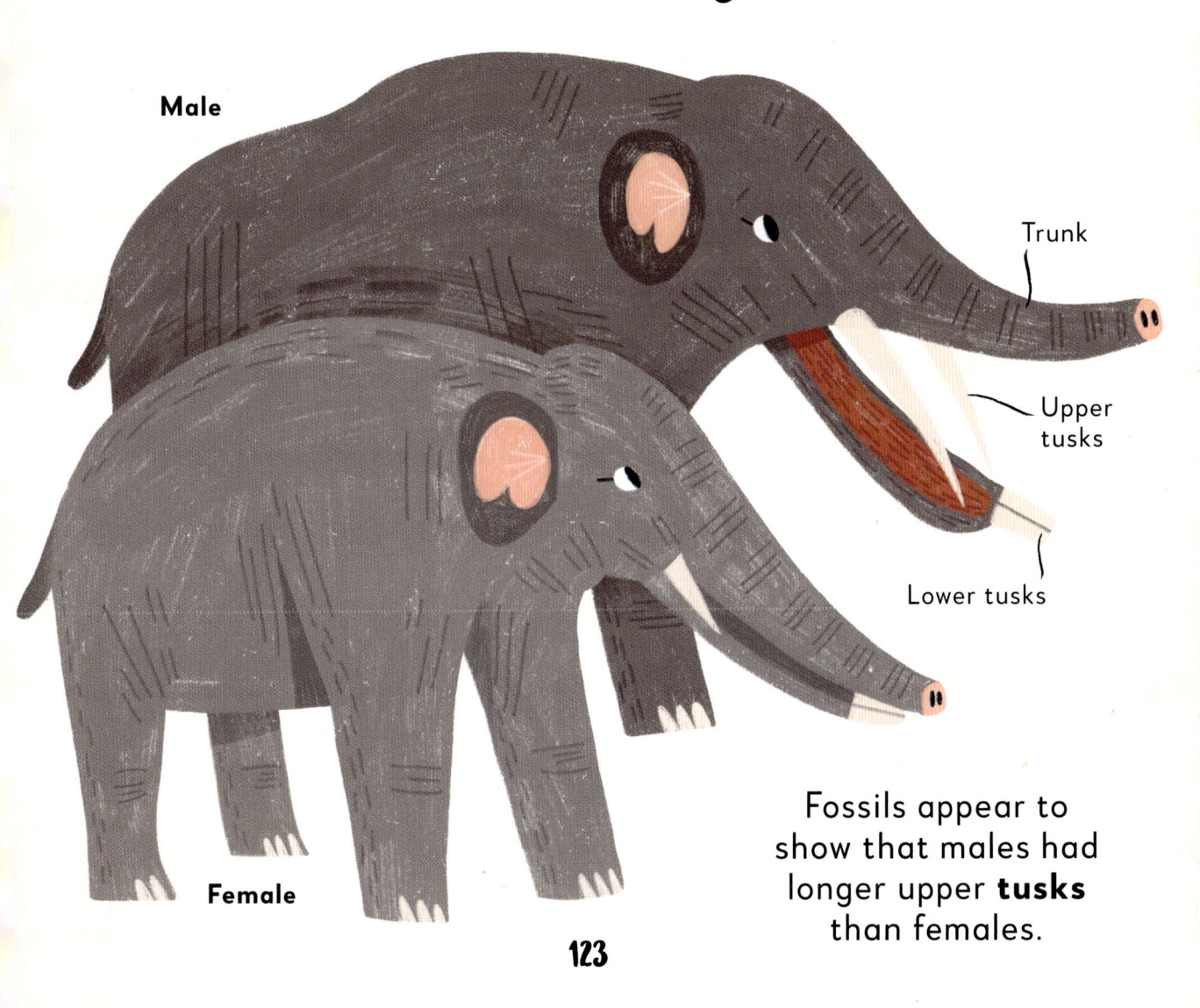

Male

Trunk

Upper tusks

Lower tusks

Female

Fossils appear to show that males had longer upper **tusks** than females.

Neogene

Ceratogaulus
(seh-rat-oh-GOR-luss)

Nicknamed the **horned gopher**, this badger-sized mammal was a rodent, like squirrels and mice. It is the only rodent known to have **horns**.

Small eyes

Two horns

The **horns** were used for defence against attackers and to show off.

Sharp **claws** were used for digging in the dirt and making holes.

Long neck

Macrauchenia may have had a short **trunk**.

Long legs

Macrauchenia
(ma-kroh-KEE-nee-a)

Was it a **llama** or a camel? No, this mammal was more closely related to horses. A **long** neck allowed it to reach both grass and high-up leaves.

Quaternary

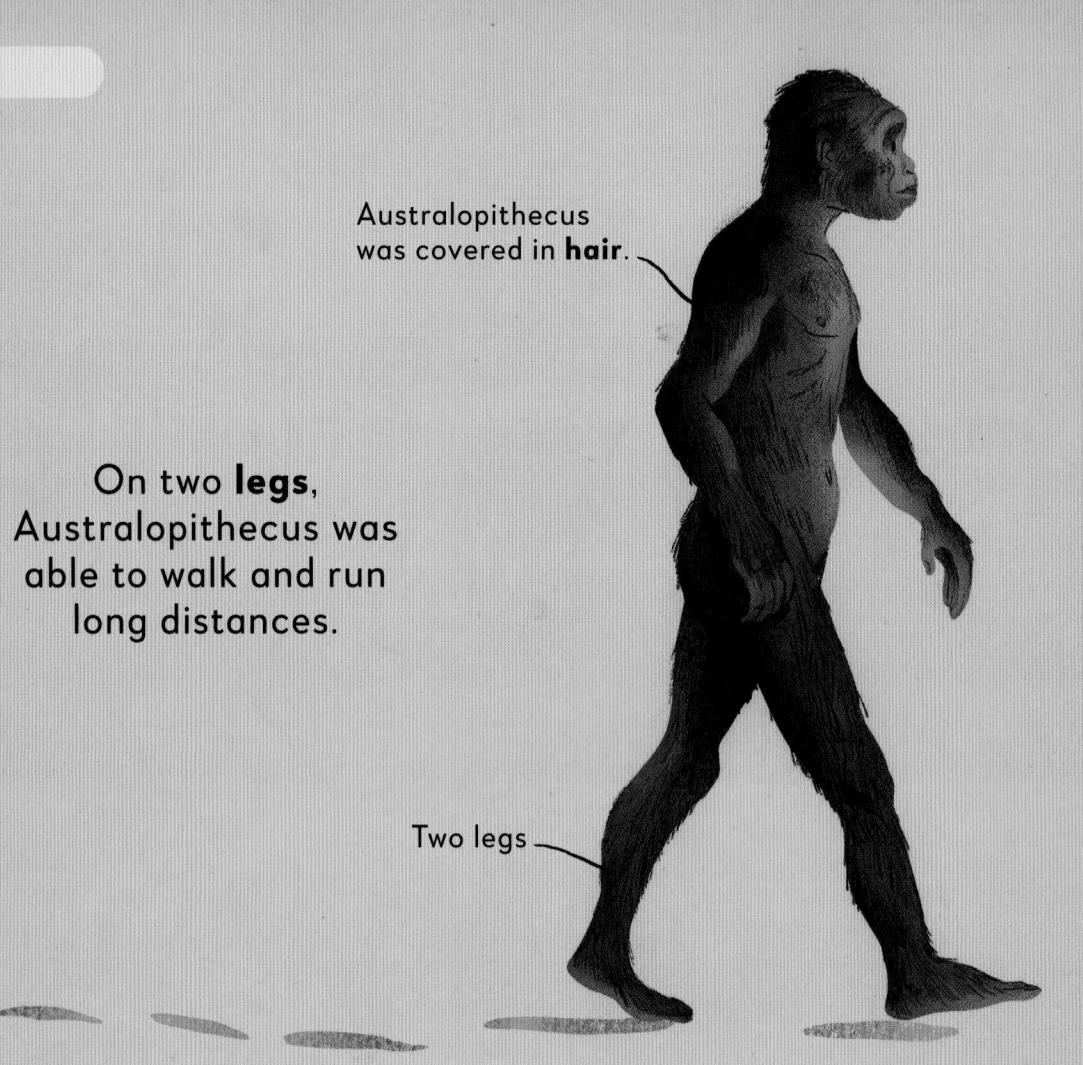

Australopithecus was covered in **hair**.

On two **legs**, Australopithecus was able to walk and run long distances.

Two legs

Australopithecus

(o-stral-oh-PITH-i-kuss)

Australopithecus was an **early** relative of humans. It appeared about 4 million years ago and walked on two legs. It even left behind fossil **footprints**.

Glyptodon was a car-sized cousin of armadillos!

Tough shell

Armoured tail

Claws

Glyptodon

(GLIP-toh-don)

A thick, domed shell made up of solid bone **tiles** helped to protect this mammal from hungry predators. It became **extinct** a little over 10,000 years ago.

Quaternary

Smilodon

(SMY-loh-don)

This big kitty is also known as the sabre-toothed cat due to its two teeth that looked like **swords**. It was a fearsome hunter.

Huge teeth

Short tail

Smilodon was an expert at surprise attacks. It **pounced** on prey then wrestled it to the ground. Finally, it delivered a deadly bite with its enormous fangs.

Smilodon preyed on mammals, such as small mammoths.

Smilodon's extra large **teeth** were almost 30 cm (1 ft) long.

Claws

Quaternary

Thylacoleo
(thy-la-koh-LEE-oh)

This prowling animal was a type of mammal called a **marsupial**, like kangaroos and koalas. A **fierce** hunter, it had a powerful bite as strong as a lion's.

Thylacoleo carried its young inside a snug pouch on its belly.

A long **tail** helped Thylacoleo to balance.

Sharp **teeth**

A large **thumb claw** was used as a weapon.

Short snout

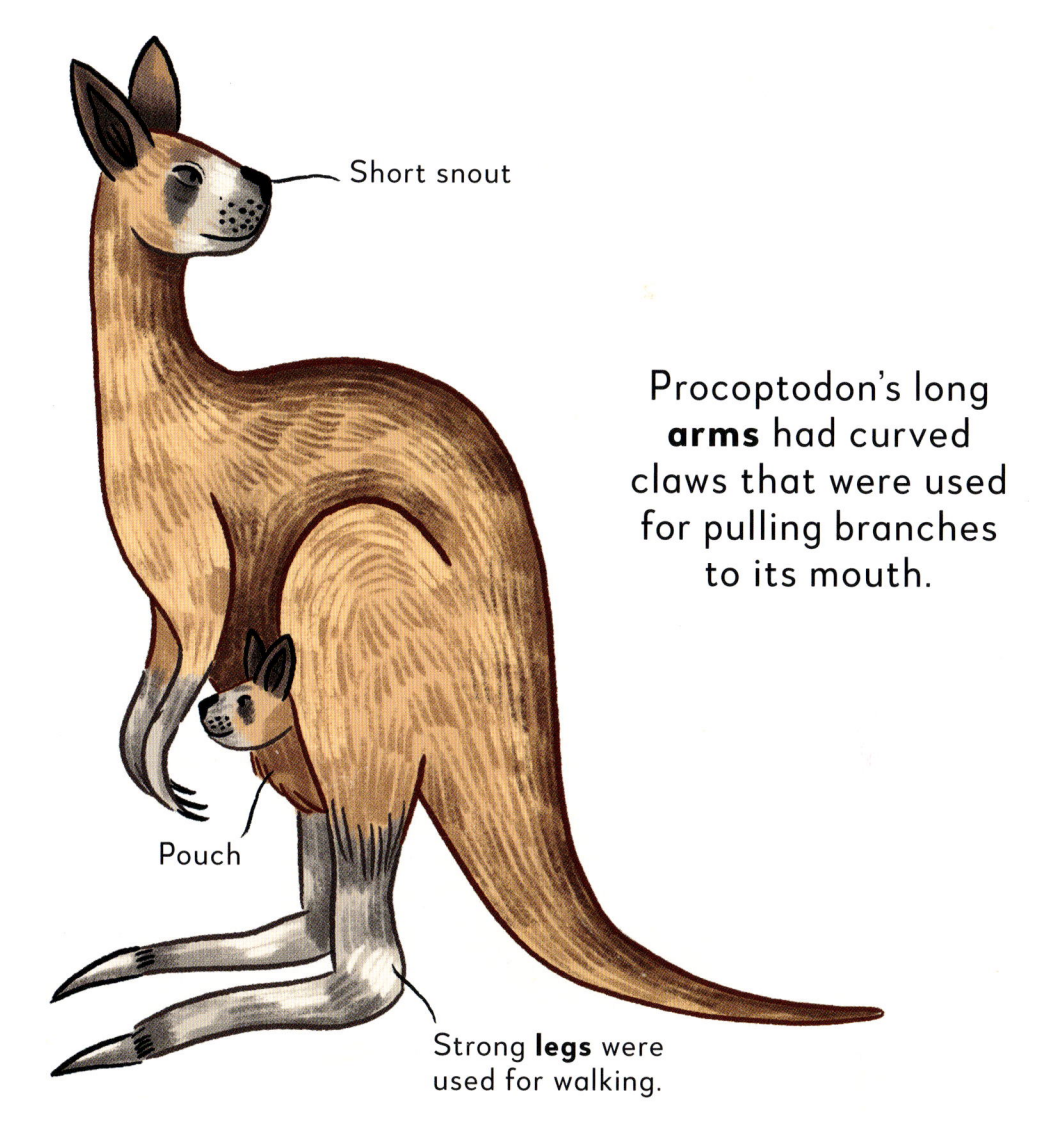

Procoptodon's long **arms** had curved claws that were used for pulling branches to its mouth.

Pouch

Strong **legs** were used for walking.

Procoptodon
(proh-KOP-toh-don)

As tall as a door, this was the largest and **heaviest** kangaroo that ever existed. At almost three times the size of the biggest living kangaroo, it was too heavy to **hop**.

Quaternary

Powerful body

Short snout

Long legs meant Arctodus was a fast **runner**.

Arctodus

(ark-TOH-duss)

Arctodus was the biggest bear that has ever lived. Standing on its back legs, it would have **towered** over a human. It wasn't a fussy eater, **gobbling** up meat, plants, and fruit.

Mylodon

(MAI-loh-don)

You might be surprised to discover that this furry giant was a close cousin of today's **sloths**. While sloths live in trees, Mylodon was too big to climb and lived in **caves**.

Mylodon was about the size of an elephant.

Long snout

Thick fur

Large **claws** were used for digging in the ground and grabbing fruit and leaves.

Quaternary

Diprotodon
(dai-PROH-toh-don)

This was a bull-sized cousin of the wombat. It is the largest known **marsupial** ever and lived in Australia. Marsupials are mammals that keep their young in **pouches**.

Bulky body

Sharp front teeth

Each year, herds of Diprotodon moved long distances, or **migrated**, to find food.

Ancient bison

This is an Ice Age **relative** of the American bison found today in North America. It was a large plant eater that dined on grass and **roamed** in huge herds.

A big **hump** supported powerful muscles that helped the ancient bison to hold up its large head.

Large horns

Strong body

Quaternary

Woolly mammoth

With its bulky body and big **tusks**, this animal could be mistaken for an elephant wearing a woolly coat! Shaggy hair kept this mammoth **warm** in cold weather.

The shaggy coat had three different layers of **fur**.

Giant tusks

Trunk

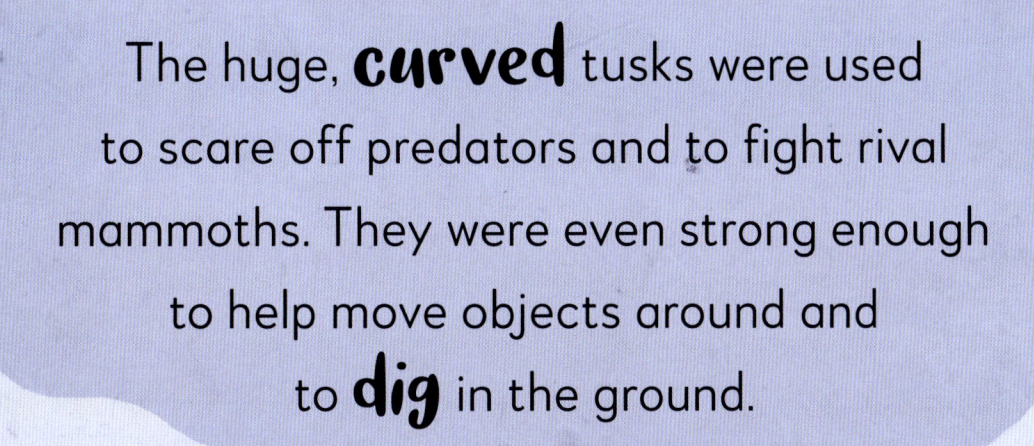

The huge, **curved** tusks were used to scare off predators and to fight rival mammoths. They were even strong enough to help move objects around and to **dig** in the ground.

Woolly mammoths were still **alive** when the ancient Egyptians built the Great Pyramid at Giza about 4,600 years ago.

Mammoths lived in large herds for safety.

Quaternary

Ice Age steppe

During the Ice Age, some parts of the world were much **chillier** than today. The open land known as steppe was filled with **grass** and was home to all sorts of mammals.

To escape the freezing weather, these lions lived in **caves**.

Cave lion

This rhinoceros had a giant **horn** longer than a baseball bat.

Woolly rhinoceros

To survive the cold, Ice Age animals needed warm fur.

Male giant deer had huge **antlers** that were wider than four doorways.

Giant deer

Early humans **hunted** large plant-eating animals with weapons made from stone.

Early humans

Glossary

armour
Protective layer or shell that covers an animal, such as an alligator's hard scales

backbone
Spine of an animal

beak
Hard, pointed part of an animal's mouth, used for picking up food

burrow
Hole or tunnel dug by an animal

claw
Curved nail on the end of a finger or toe

crest
Part of an animal found on its head, made of skin, feathers, or bone that is used for showing off

extinct
Description of an animal or plant that no longer exists

feeler
Slender body part found on the head of an animal that is used for feeling or sensing

fin
Thin, flat limb used for swimming, such as a fish's fins

flipper
Flat limb used for swimming, such as a whale's flippers

fossil
Remains or traces of an ancient animal or plant, often made from rock

frill
Sheet of bone that protected the neck of a dinosaur, such as Triceratops

herd
Large group of animals that live together

hoof
Large, strong toenail, such as a horse's hooves

horn
Hard, often curved, spike found on the head of an animal, such as a rhino's horns

insect
Small animal with six legs, such as an ant or fly

jaws
Moveable parts of an animal's mouth that allow it to bite

nest
Home made by an animal to lay its eggs in, such as a bird's nest

plate
Sheet of bone found on the back of a dinosaur, such as Stegosaurus

predator
Animal that eats other animals for food

prey
Animal that is hunted by another animal for food

scales
Small, hard plates covering the skin of an animal

shell
Hard, protective covering of an animal, such as a turtle's shell

spine
Thin, sharp spike that sticks out of an animal's skin or shell for protection

swamp
Flooded area filled with trees and plants

tentacle
Bendy arm-like limb of an animal used for catching food and for feeling

tusk
Huge, pointed tooth, such as an elephant's tusks

webbed feet
Feet with toes joined together by skin, such as a duck's, to help with swimming

Prehistoric A-Z

Aa
Albertonectes 95
Ambulocetus 110
Amphicyon 120
Ancient bison 135
Andrewsarchus 113
Anomalocaris 19
Anthropornis 115
Archaeanthus 83
Archaeopteris 31
Archaeopteryx 69
Archelon 93
Arctodus 132
Argentinosaurus 85
Arthropleura 36–37
Asterolepis 31
Astraspis 21
Attercopus 27
Australopithecus 126

Bb
Banksia archaeocarpa.... 111
Baryonyx 76
Basilosaurus 114
Brachiosaurus 70–71

Cc
Calamites 34
Cave lion 138
Ceratogaulus 124
Chalicotherium 122

Changmiania 82
Charnia 12
Citipati 94
Coelophysis 52–53
Compsognathus 69
Confuciusornis 79
Cooksonia 22
Crioceratites 73
Cryolophosaurus 59
Cylindroteuthis... 62–63

Dd
Dactylioceras 60
Deinocheirus 99
Deinosuchus 87
Dickinsonia 13
Didymograptus 20
Dilophosaurus 56
Dimetrodon 40
Diplodocus 66–67
Diprotodon 134
Dunkleosteus 29

Ee
Edaphosaurus 39
Einiosaurus 96
Elginia 43
Elrathia 15
Eodromaeus 49
Eoraptor 51
Eosimias 112
Euoplocephalus 90

Eurypterus 23
Eusthenopteron 28

Gg
Gallimimus 98
Gastornis 116
Giant deer 139
Glyptodon 127

Hh
Haikouichthys 14
Hallucigenia 17
Herrerasaurus 48
Heterodontosaurus ... 57
Hyperodapedon 49

Ii
Icaronycteris 109
Ichthyosaurus 54–55
Ichthyostega 32
Iguanodon 75
Indosuchus 100

Ll
Laccognathus 30
Lambeosaurus 91
Lepidotes 61
Liopleurodon 62–63

Mm
Macrauchenia 125
Maiasaura 88–89
Mamenchisaurus 65

Marrella 18
Megalodon 121
Meganeura 38
Megazostrodon 58
Mei 77
Mesohippus 117
Mesolimulus 68
Mesonyx 117
Mosasaurus 97
Mucrospirifer 26
Muttaburrasaurus 84
Mylodon 133

Nn
Nothosaurus 46

Oo
Opabinia 16
Ottoia 19

Pp
Pachycephalosaurus ......
   102
Palaeocastor 119
Paraceratherium 118
Pikaia 19
Platybelodon 123
Polacanthus 74
Postosuchus 52–53
Procoptodon 131
Psittacosaurus 79
Pterodactylus 68
Pterodaustro 80–81

Qq
Quetzalcoatlus 101

Rr
Repenomamus 78
Rhamphorhynchus 69

Ss
Saurosuchus 48
Scutosaurus 42
Seymouria 41
Shonisaurus 50
Sinosauropteryx 78
Smilodon 128–129
Spinosaurus 86
Stagonolepis 47
Stegosaurus ....
   66–67, 72
Stethacanthus 33

Tt
Thylacoleo 130
Tiktaalik 31
Titanoboa 108
Triceratops ....
   96, 103, 104
Tyrannosaurus ....
   104–105

Uu
Uintatherium 116

Vv
Velociraptor 77, 92

Ww
Walliserops 25
Wiwaxia 18
Woodocrinus 35
Woolly mammoth ....
   136–137
Woolly rhinoceros ....
   138
Wuerhosaurus 72

Yy
Yi 64

Zz
Zenaspis 24

Author Dr Dean Lomax
Illustrators Jean Claude, Kaja Kajfež, Marc Pattenden, Sara Ugolotti

Project editor Olivia Stanford
Designer Holly Price
Additional design Sonny Flynn
Managing editors Marie Greenwood, Jonathan Melmoth
Managing art editor Diane Peyton Jones
Jacket designer Elle Ward
Jacket coordinator Magda Pszuk
Production editor Dragana Puvacic
Senior production controller Inderjit Bhullar
Deputy art director Mabel Chan
Publishing director Sarah Larter

This edition published in 2024
First published in Great Britain in 2023 by
Dorling Kindersley Limited
DK, One Embassy Gardens, 8 Viaduct Gardens,
London SW11 7BW

The authorised representative in the EEA is
Dorling Kindersley Verlag GmbH. Arnulfstr. 124,
80636 Munich, Germany

Copyright © 2024 Dorling Kindersley Limited
A Penguin Random House Company
10 9 8 7 6 5 4 3 2
002–340599–Aug/2024

All rights reserved.
No part of this publication may be reproduced, stored in or introduced into a retrieval system, or transmitted, in any form, or by any means (electronic, mechanical, photocopying, recording, or otherwise), without the prior written permission of the copyright owner.

A CIP catalogue record for this book is available from the British Library.
ISBN: 978-0-2416-6989-1

Printed and bound in China

www.dk.com

Acknowledgements

Dr Dean Lomax would like to dedicate this book to his friend and fellow paleontologist, Jason Sherburn, who he hopes will enjoy reading this book with his nephew. He would also like to thank Natalie Turner for her help.

DK would like to thank: Rebecca Arlington and Kathleen Teece for editorial assistance; Sif Nørskov for design assistance; and Caroline Hunt for proofreading.

Paleogeography globes derived from original maps produced by Colorado Plateau Geosystems Inc.

Picture credits
1–144 123RF.com: laurent davoust for background texture

All other images © Dorling Kindersley

This book was made with Forest Stewardship Council™ certified paper – one small step in DK's commitment to a sustainable future. Learn more at www.dk.com/uk/information/sustainability

FSC® C018179